D0821555

Selected Poems

1951-1974

CHARLES TOMLINSON

Selected Poems

1951-1974

OXFORD LONDON NEW YORK
OXFORD UNIVERSITY PRESS
1978

Oxford University Press, Walton Street, Oxford OX2 6DP

OXFORD LONDON GLASGOW
NEW YORK TORONTO MELBOURNE WELLINGTON
IBADAN NAIROBI DAR ES SALAAM CAPE TOWN
KUALA LUMPUR SINGAPORE JAKARTA HONG KONG TOKYO
DELHI BOMBAY CALCUTTA MADRAS KARACHI

British Library Cataloguing in Publication Data

Tomlinson, Charles
Selected poems, 1951–1974.
I. Title
821'.9'14 PR6039.0349 77–30466

ISBN 0–19–211882–X
ISBN 0–19–211883–8 Pbk.

PRINTED IN GREAT BRITAIN BY
THE BOWERING PRESS LTD, PLYMOUTH

TO BRENDA

CONTENTS

WRITTEN ON WATER (1972)

THE WAY IN (1974)

NOTES

'Over Brooklyn Bridge' (p. 54) 'The poet cedes his elocutionary function . . .' is a slightly travestied version of a famous passage from Mallarmé's *Crise de vers*: 'l'œuvre pure implique la disparition élocutoire du poète, qui cède l'initiative aux mots. . . .'

'Prometheus' (p. 86) refers to the tone-poem by Scriabin and to his hope of transforming the world by music and rite.

'Ariadne and the Minotaur' (p. 120) Suggested initially by Picasso's series of drawings, this ignores as they do the question of the actual kinship between Ariadne and the Minotaur. Perhaps she, too, was unaware of it.

'Over Elizabeth Bridge' (p. 126) László Rajk, Hungarian Foreign Minister, executed during the Stalinist period; Imre Nagy, Prime Minister and leader of the 1956 revolution, also executed. The poet, Attila József, killed himself in the thirties.

Selected Poems

POEM

Wakening with the window over fields,
To the coin-clear harness-jingle as a float
Clips by, and each succeeding hoof fall, now remote,
Breaks clean and frost-sharp on the unstopped ear.

The hooves describe an arabesque on space,
A dotted line in sound that falls and rises
As the cart goes by, recedes, turns to retrace
Its way back through the unawakened village.

And space vibrates, enlarges with the sound;
Though space is soundless, yet creates
From very soundlessness a ground
To counterstress the lilting hoof fall as it breaks.

AESTHETIC

Reality is to be sought, not in concrete,
But in space made articulate:
The shore, for instance,
Spreading between wall and wall;
The sea-voice
Tearing the silence from the silence.

VENICE

Cut into by doors
The morning assumes night's burden,
The houses assemble in tight cubes.

From the palace flanking the waterfront
She is about to embark, but pauses.
Her dress is a veil of sound
Extended upon silence.

Under the bridge,
Contained by the reflected arc
A tunnel of light
Effaces walls, water, horizon.

Floating upon its own image
A cortège of boats idles through space.

NINE VARIATIONS
IN A CHINESE WINTER SETTING

I

Warm flute on the cold snow
Lays amber in sound.

II

Against brushed cymbal
Grounds yellow on green,
Amber on tinkling ice.

III

The sage beneath the waterfall
Numbers the blessing of a flute;
Water lets down
Exploding silk.

IV

The hiss of raffia,
The thin string scraped with the back of the bow
Are not more bat-like
Than the gusty bamboos
Against a flute.

V

Pine-scent
In snow-clearness
Is not more exactly counterpointed
Than the creak of trodden snow
Against a flute.

VI

The outline of the water-dragon
Is not embroidered with so intricate a thread
As that with which the flute
Defines the tangible borders of a mood.

VII

The flute in summer makes streams of ice:
In winter it grows hospitable.

VIII

In mist, also, a flute is cold
Beside a flute in snow.

IX

Degrees of comparison
Go with differing conditions:
Sunlight mellows lichens,
Whereas snow mellows the flute.

SUGGESTIONS FOR THE IMPROVEMENT OF A SUNSET

Darkening the edges of the land,
Imperceptibly it must drain out colours
Drawing all light into its centre.

Six points of vantage provide us with six sunsets.

The sea partakes of the sky. It is less
Itself than the least pool which, if threatened,
Prizes lucidity.

The pond is lime-green, an enemy
Of gold, bearing no change but shadow.

Seen from above, the house would resemble
A violin, abandoned, and lost in its own darkness;

Diminished, through the wrong end of a glass,
A dice ambushed by lowering greens;

Accorded its true proportions,
The stone would give back the light
Which, all day, it has absorbed.

The after-glow, broken by leaves and windows,
Confirms green's triumph against yellow.

SEA CHANGE

To define the sea—
We change our opinions
With the changing light.

Light struggles with colour:
A quincunx
Of five stones, a white
Opal threatened by emeralds.

The sea is uneasy marble.

The sea is green silk.

The sea is blue mud, churned
By the insistence of wind.

Beneath dawn a sardonyx may be cut from it
In white layers laced with a carnelian orange,
A leek- or apple-green chalcedony
Hewn in the cold light.

Illustration is white wine
Floating in a saucer of ground glass
On a pedestal of cut glass:

A static instance, therefore, untrue.

THROUGH BINOCULARS

In their congealed light
We discover that what we had taken for a face
Has neither eyes nor mouth,
But only the impersonality of anatomy.

Silencing movement,
They withdraw life.

Definition grows clear-cut, but bodiless,
Withering by a dimension.

To see thus
Is to ignore the revenge of light on shadow,
To confound both in a brittle and false union.

This fictive extension into madness
Has a kind of bracing effect:
That normality is, after all, desirable
One can no longer doubt having experienced its opposite.

Binoculars are the last phase in a romanticism:
The starkly mad vision, not mortal,
But dangling one in a vicarious, momentary idiocy.

To dispense with them
Is to make audible the steady roar of evening,
Withdrawing in slow ripples of orange,
Like the retreat of water from sea-caves.

DIALOGUE

She: It turns on its axis.

He: To say that it was round
Would be to ignore what is within.
The transparent framework of cells,
The constellation of flashes.

She: It reveals the horizon.

He: It surrounds it,
Transmits and refines it
Through a frozen element:
A taut line crossing a pure white.

She: It contains distance.

He: It distances what is near,
Transforms the conversation piece
Into a still life,
Isolates, like the end of a corridor.

She: It is the world of contour:

He: The black outline separating brilliances
That would otherwise fuse,
A single flame.

She: If it held personages—

He: They would be minute,
Their explicit movements
The mosaic which dances.

Both: In unison, they would clarify
The interior of the fruit,
The heart of the cut stone.

FLUTE MUSIC

There is a moment for speech and for silence.
Lost between possibilities
But deploring a forced harmony,
We elect the flute.

A season, defying gloss, may be the sum
Of blue water beneath green rain;
It may comprise comets, days, lakes
Yet still bear the exegesis of music.

Seeing and speaking we are two men:
The eye encloses as a window—a flute
Governs the land, its winter and its silence.

The flute is uncircumscribed by moonlight or irised mornings.
It moves with equal certainty
Through a register of palm-greens and flesh-rose.

The glare of brass over a restless bass
(Red glow across olive twilight)
Urges to a delighted excess,
A weeping among broken gods.

The flute speaks (reason's song
Riding the ungovernable wave)
The bound of passion
Out of the equitable core of peace.

THE ART OF POETRY

At first, the mind feels bruised.
The light makes white holes through the black foliage
Or mist hides everything that is not itself.

But how shall one say so?—
The fact being, that when the truth is not good enough
We exaggerate. Proportions

Matter. It is difficult to get them right.
There must be nothing
Superfluous, nothing which is not elegant
And nothing which is if it is merely that.

This green twilight has violet borders.

Yellow butterflies
Nervously transferring themselves
From scarlet to bronze flowers
Disappear as the evening appears.

OBSERVATION OF FACTS

Facts have no eyes. One must
Surprise them, as one surprises a tree
By regarding its (shall I say?)
Facets of copiousness.

The tree stands.

The house encloses.

The room flowers.

These are fact stripped of imagination:
Their relation is mutual.

A dryad is a sort of chintz curtain
Between myself and a tree.
The tree stands: or does not stand:
As I draw, or remove the curtain.

The house encloses: or fails to signify
As being bodied over against one,
As something one has to do with.

The room flowers once one has introduced
Mental fibre beneath its elegance,
A rough pot or two, outweighing
The persistence of frippery
In lampshades or wallpaper.

Style speaks what was seen,
Or it conceals the observation
Behind the observer: a voice
Wearing a ruff.

Those facets of copiousness which I proposed
Exist, do so when we have silenced ourselves.

FIASCHERINO

Over an ash-fawn beach fronting a sea which keeps
  Rolling and unrolling, lifting
The green fringes from submerged rocks
  On its way in, and, on its way out
Dropping them again, the light

Squanders itself, a saffron morning
  Advances among foam and stones, sticks
Clotted with black naphtha
  And frayed to the newly carved
Fresh white of chicken flesh.

One leans from the cliff-top. Height
  Distances like an inverted glass; the shore
Is diminished but concentrated, jewelled
  With the clarity of warm colours
That, seen more nearly, would dissipate

Into masses. The map-like interplay
  Of sea-light against shadow
And the mottled close-up of wet rocks
  Drying themselves in the hot air
Are lost to us. Content with our portion,

Where, we ask ourselves, is the end of all this
  Variety that follows us? Glare
Pierces muslin; its broken rays
  Hovering in trembling filaments
Glance on the ceiling with no more substance

Than a bee's wing. Thickening, these
  Hang down over the pink walls
In green bars, and flickering between them,
  A moving fan of two colours,
The sea unrolls and rolls itself into the low room.

THE ATLANTIC

Launched into an opposing wind, hangs
  Grappled beneath the onrush,
And there, lifts, curling in spume,
  Unlocks, drops from that hold
Over and shoreward. The beach receives it,
  A whitening line, collapsing
Powdering-off down its broken length;
  Then, curded, shallow, heavy
With clustering bubbles, it nears
  In a slow sheet that must climb
Relinquishing its power, upward
  Across tilted sand. Unravelled now
And the shore, under its lucid pane,
  Clear to the sight, it is spent:
The sun rocks there, as the netted ripple
  Into whose skeins the motion threads it
Glances athwart a bed, honey-combed
  By heaving stones. Neither survives the instant
But is caught back, and leaves, like the after-image
  Released from the floor of a now different mind,
A quick gold, dyeing the uncovering beach
  With sunglaze. That which we were,
Confronted by all that we are not,
  Grasps in subservience its replenishment.

WINTER ENCOUNTERS

House and hollow; village and valley-side:
  The ceaseless pairings, the interchange
In which the properties are constant
  Resumes its winter starkness. The hedges' barbs
Are bared. Lengthened shadows
  Intersecting, the fields seem parcelled smaller
As if by hedgerow within hedgerow. Meshed
  Into neighbourhood by such shifting ties,
The house reposes, squarely upon its acre
  Yet with softened angles, the responsive stone

Changeful beneath the changing light:
  There is a riding-forth, a voyage impending
In this ruffled air, where all moves
  Towards encounter. Inanimate or human,
The distinction fails in these brisk exchanges—
  Say, merely, that the roof greets the cloud,
Or by the wall, sheltering its knot of talkers,
  Encounter enacts itself in the conversation
On customary subjects, where the mind
  May lean at ease, weighing the prospect
Of another's presence. Rain
  And the probability of rain, tares
And their progress through a field of wheat—
  These, though of moment in themselves,
Serve rather to articulate the sense
  That having met, one meets with more
Than the words can witness. One feels behind
  Into the intensity that bodies through them
Calmness within the wind, the warmth in cold.

OXEN: PLOUGHING AT FIESOLE

The heads, impenetrable
And the slow bulk
Soundless and stooping,
A white darkness—burdened
Only by sun, and not
By the matchwood yoke—
They groove in ease
The meadow through which they pace
Tractable. It is as if
Fresh from the escape,
They consent to submission,
The debris of captivity
Still clinging there
Unnoticed behind those backs:
'But we submit'—the tenor
Unambiguous in that stride
Of even confidence—
'Giving and not conceding

Your premises. Work
Is necessary, therefore—'
(With an unsevered motion
Holding the pauses
Between stride and stride)
'We will be useful
But we will not be swift: now
Follow us for your improvement
And at our pace.' This calm
Bred from this strength, and the reality
Broaching no such discussion,
The man will follow, each
As the other's servant
Content to remain content.

THE MEDITERRANEAN

I

In this country of grapes
Where the architecture
Plays musical interludes, flays
The emotions with the barest statement
Or, confusing the issue and the beholder,
Bewilders with an excessive formality,
There is also the sea.

II

The sea
Whether it is 'wrinkled' and 'crawls'
Or pounds, plunders, rounding
On itself in thunderous showers, a
Broken, bellowing foam canopy
Rock-riven and driven wild
By its own formless griefs—the sea
Carries, midway, its burning stripe of light.

III

This country of grapes
Is a country, also, of trains, planes and gasworks.
'Tramway and palace' rankles. It is an idea
Neither the guidebook nor the imagination
Tolerates. The guidebook half lies
Of 'twenty minutes in a comfortable bus'
Of 'rows of cypresses, an
Uninterrupted series of matchless sights'.
The imagination cannot lie. It bites brick;
Says: 'This is steel—I will taste steel.
Bred on a lie, I am merely
Guidebooks, advertisements, politics.'

The sea laps by the railroad tracks.
To have admitted this also defines the sea.

ICOS

White, a shingled path
Climbs among dusted olives
To where at the hill-crest
Stare houses, whiter
Than either dust or shingle.
The view, held from this vantage
Unsoftened by distance, because
Scoured by a full light,
Draws lucid across its depth
The willing eye: a beach,
A surf-line, broken
Where reefs meet it, into the heaving
Blanched rims of bay-arcs;
Above, piercing the empty blue,
A gull would convey whiteness
Through the sole space which lacks it
But, there, scanning the shore,
Hangs only the eagle, depth
Measured within its level gaze.

HOW STILL THE HAWK

How still the hawk
Hangs innocent above
Its native wood:
Distance, that purifies the act
Of all intent, has graced
Intent with beauty.
Beauty must lie
As innocence must harm
Whose end (sited,
Held) is naked
Like the map it cowers on.
And the doom drops:
Plummet of peace
To him who does not share
The nearness and the need,
The shrivelled circle
Of magnetic fear.

GLASS GRAIN

The glare goes down. The metal of a molten pane
Cast on the wall with red light burning through,
Holds in its firm, disordered square, the shifting strands
The glass conceals, till (splitting sun) it dances
Lanterns in lanes of light its own streaked image.
Like combed-down hair. Like weathered wood, where
Line, running with, crowds on line and swaying
Rounding each knot, yet still keeps keen
The perfect parallel. Like . . . in likes, what do we look for?
Distinctions? That, but not that in sum. Think of the fugue's
 theme:
After inversions and divisions, doors
That no keys can open, cornered conceits
Apprehensions, all ways of knowledge past,
Eden comes round again, the motive dips
Back to its shapely self, its naked nature
Clothed by comparison alone—related. We ask

No less, watching suggestions that a beam selects
From wood, from water, from a muslin-weave,
Swerving across our window, on our wall
(Transparency teased out) the grain of glass.

TRAMONTANA AT LERICI

Today, should you let fall a glass it would
  Disintegrate, played off with such keenness
Against the cold's resonance (the sounds
  Hard, separate and distinct, dropping away
In a diminishing cadence) that you might swear
  This was the imitation of glass falling.

Leaf-dapples sharpen. Emboldened by this clarity
  The minds of artificers would turn prismatic,
Running on lace perforated in crisp wafers
  That could cut like steel. Constitutions,
Drafted under this fecund chill, would be annulled
  For the strictness of their equity, the moderation of their pity.

At evening, one is alarmed by such definition
  In as many lost greens as one will give glances to recover,
As many again which the landscape
  Absorbing into the steady dusk, condenses
From aquamarine to that slow indigo-pitch
  Where the light and twilight abandon themselves.

And the chill grows. In this air
  Unfit for politicians and romantics
Dark hardens from blue, effacing the windows:
  A tangible block, it will be no accessory
To that which does not concern it. One is ignored
  By so much cold suspended in so much night.

NORTHERN SPRING

Nor is this the setting for extravagance. Trees
  Fight with the wind, the wind eludes them
Streaking its cross-lanes over the uneasy water
  Whose bronze whitens. To emulate such confusion
One must impoverish the resources of folly,
  But to taste it is medicinal. Consider

How through that broken calm, as the sun emerges,
  The sky flushes its blue, dyeing the grass
In the promise of a more stable tone:
  Less swift however than the cloud is wide—
Its shadow (already) quenching the verdure
  As its bulk muffles the sun—the blue drains
And the assault renews in colourless ripples.

Then, lit, the scene deepens. Where should one look
  In the profusion of possibilities? One conceives
Placing before them a square house
  Washed in the coolness of lime, a hub
For the scattered deployment, to define
  In pure white from its verdant ground
The variegated excess which threatens it.

Spring lours. Neither will the summer achieve
  That Roman season of an equable province
Where the sun is its own witness and the shadow
  Measures its ardour with the impartiality
Of the just. Evening, debauching this sky, asks
  To be appraised and to be withstood.

THE GORGE

Wind in the fleece of ivy
As, from above, the pilot
Sees water, moved by its currents.

But we are closer: he would miss
Such evident ripples
Like a conflagration
Climbing the rockface.

Light, swept perpendicular
Into the leaf-mass
Flickers out, only to reappear momentarily
Stippling remoter clumps.

The movement deceives, a surface
For silence, inaccessible
Inactivity. Even the sea
Shifts to its centre.

ON A LANDSCAPE BY LI CH'ENG

Look down. There is snow.
Where the snow ends
Sea, and where the sea enters
Grey among capes
Like an unvaried sky, lapping
From finger to finger
Of a raised hand, travellers
Skirt between snow and sea.
Minute, furtive and exposed,
Their solitude is unchosen and will end
In comity, in talk
So seasoned by these extremes
It will recall stored fruits
Bitten by a winter fire.
The title, without disapprobation,
Says 'Merchants.'

THE CRANE

That insect, without antennae, over its
Cotton-spool lip, letting
An almost invisible tenuity
Of steel cable, drop
Some seventy feet, with the
Grappling hook hidden also
Behind a dense foreground
Among which it is fumbling, and
Over which, mantis-like
It is begging or threatening, gracile
From a clear sky—that paternal
Constructive insect, without antennae,
Would seem to assure us that
'The future is safe, because
It is in my hands.' And we do not
Doubt this veracity, we can only
Fear it—as many of us
As pause here to remark
Such silent solicitude
For lifting intangible weights
Into real walls.

PARING THE APPLE

There are portraits and still-lives.

And there is paring the apple.

And then? Paring it slowly,
From under cool-yellow
Cold-white emerging. And . . .?

The spring of concentric peel
Unwinding off white,
The blade hidden, dividing.

There are portraits and still-lives
And the first, because 'human'
Does not excel the second, and
Neither is less weighted
With a human gesture, than paring the apple
With a human stillness.

The cool blade
Severs between coolness, apple-rind
Compelling a recognition.

ROSE-HIPS

Weather the frost, stir
At the cold's passing
Where white alone (were it not
For such drops of fire)
Would dominate, as the incessant
Massing of mist on mist
Draws-to over distance, leaving
Only a white of frost
On a white of fog, but
Deepened in dye by such
Candid obscurity, they stare
Sharper than summer berries
From this unlit air.

MORE FOREIGN CITIES

'Nobody wants any more poems about foreign cities. . . .'
(From a recent disquisition on poetics)

Not forgetting Ko-jen, that
Musical city (it has
Few buildings and annexes
Space by combating silence),

There is Fiordiligi, its sun-changes
Against walls of transparent stone
Unsettling all preconception—a city
For architects (they are taught
By casting their nets
Into those moving shoals); and there is
Kairouan, whose lit space
So slides into and fits
The stone masses, one would doubt
Which was the more solid
Unless, folding back
Gold segments out of the white
Pith globe of a quartered orange,
One may learn perhaps
To read such perspectives. At Luna
There is a city of bridges, where
Even the inhabitants are mindful
Of a shared privilege: a bridge
Does not exist for its own sake.
It commands vacancy.

A MEDITATION ON JOHN CONSTABLE

'Painting is a science, and should be pursued as an inquiry into the laws of nature. Why, then, may not landscape painting be considered as a branch of natural philosophy, of which pictures are but the experiments?'

(JOHN CONSTABLE, *The History of Landscape Painting*)

He replied to his own question, and with the unmannered
  Exactness of art; enriched his premises
By confirming his practice: the labour of observation
  In face of meteorological fact. Clouds
Followed by others, temper the sun in passing
  Over and off it. Massed darks
Blotting it back, scattered and mellowed shafts
  Break damply out of them, until the source
Unmasks, floods its retreating bank
  With raw fire. One perceives (though scarcely)
The remnant clouds trailing across it
  In rags, and thinned to a gauze.

But the next will dam it. They loom past
  And narrow its blaze. It shrinks to a crescent
Crushed out, a still lengthening ooze
  As the mass thickens, though cannot exclude
Its silvered-yellow. The eclipse is sudden,
  Seen first on the darkening grass, then complete
In a covered sky.
                Facts. And what are they?
He admired accidents, because governed by laws,
  Representing them (since the illusion was not his end)
As governed by feeling. The end is our approval
  Freely accorded, the illusion persuading us
That it exists as a human image. Caught
  By a wavering sun, or under a wind
Which moistening among the outlines of banked foliage
  Prepares to dissolve them, it must grow constant;
Though there, ruffling and parted, the disturbed
  Trees let through the distance, like white fog
Into their broken ranks. It must persuade
  And with a constancy, not to be swept back
To reveal what it half-conceals. Art is itself
  Once we accept it. The day veers. He would have judged
Exactly in such a light, that strides down
  Over the quick stains of cloud-shadows
Expunged now, by its conflagration of colour.
  A descriptive painter? If delight
Describes, which wrings from the brush
  The errors of a mind, so tempered,
It can forgo all pathos; for what he saw
  Discovered what he was, and the hand—unswayed
By the dictation of a single sense—
  Bodied the accurate and total knowledge
In a calligraphy of present pleasure. Art
  Is complete when it is human. It is human
Once the looped pigments, the pin-heads of light
  Securing space under their deft restrictions
Convince, as the index of a possible passion,
  As the adequate gauge, both of the passion
And its object. The artist lies
  For the improvement of truth. Believe him.

FAREWELL TO VAN GOGH

The quiet deepens. You will not persuade
  One leaf of the accomplished, steady, darkening
Chestnut-tower to displace itself
  With more of violence than the air supplies
When, gathering dusk, the pond brims evenly
  And we must be content with stillness.

Unhastening, daylight withdraws from us its shapes
  Into their central calm. Stone by stone
Your rhetoric is dispersed until the earth
  Becomes once more the earth, the leaves
A sharp partition against cooling blue.

Farewell, and for your instructive frenzy
  Gratitude. The world does not end tonight
And the fruit that we shall pick tomorrow
  Await us, weighing the unstripped bough.

CÉZANNE AT AIX

And the mountain: each day
Immobile like fruit. Unlike, also
—Because irreducible, because
Neither a component of the delicious
And therefore questionable,
Nor distracted (as the sitter)
By his own pose and, therefore,
Doubly to be questioned: it is not
Posed. It is. Untaught
Unalterable, a stone bridgehead
To that which is tangible
Because unfelt before. There
In its weathered weight
Its silence silences, a presence
Which does not present itself.

AT HOLWELL FARM

It is a quality of air, a temperate sharpness
  Causes an autumn fire to burn compact,
To cast from a shapely and unrifted core
  Its steady brightness. A kindred flame
Gathers within the stone, and such a season
  Fosters, then frees it in a single glow:
Pears by the wall and stone as ripe as pears
  Under the shell-hood's cornice; the door's
Bright oak, the windows' slim-cut frames
  Are of an equal whiteness. Crude stone
By a canopy of shell, each complements
  In opposition, each is bound
Into a pattern of utilities—this farm
  Also a house, this house a dwelling.
Rooted in more than earth, to dwell
  Is to discern the Eden image, to grasp
In a given place and guard it well
  Shielded in stone. Whether piety
Be natural, is neither the poet's
  Nor the builder's story, but a quality of air,
Such as surrounds and shapes an autumn fire
  Bringing these sharp disparities to bear.

ON THE HALL AT STOWEY

Walking by map, I chose unwonted ground,
  A crooked, questionable path which led
Beyond the margin, then delivered me
  At a turn. Red marl
Had rutted the aimless track
  That firmly withheld the recompense it hid
Till now, close by its end, the day's discoveries
  Began with the dimming night:

A house. The wall-stones, brown.
  The doubtful light, more of a mist than light
Floating at hedge-height through the sodden fields

Had yielded, or a final glare
Burst there, rather, to concentrate
Sharp saffron, as the ebbing year—
Or so it seemed, for the dye deepened—poured
All of its yellow strength through the way I went:

Over grass, garden-space, over the grange
That jutted beyond, lengthening-down
The house line, tall as it was,
By tying it to the earth, trying its pride
(Which submitted) under a nest of barns,
A walled weight of lesser encumbrances—
Few of which worsened it, and none
As the iron sheds, sealing my own approach.

All stone. I had passed these last, unwarrantable
Symbols of—no; let me define, rather
The thing they were not, all that we cannot be,
By the description, simply of that which merits it:
Stone. Why must (as it does at each turn)
Each day, the mean rob us of patience, distract us
Before even its opposite?—before stone, which
Cut, piled, mortared, is patience's presence.

The land farmed, the house was neglected: but
Gashed panes (and there were many) still showed
Into the pride of that presence. I had reached
Unchallenged, within feet of the door
Ill-painted, but at no distant date—the least
Our prodigal time could grudge it; paused
To measure the love, to assess its object,
That trusts for continuance to the mason's hand.

Five centuries—here were (at the least) five—
In linked love, eager excrescence
Where the door, arched, crowned with acanthus,
Aimed at a civil elegance, but hit
This sturdier compromise, neither Greek, Gothic
Nor Strawberry, clumped from the arching-point
And swathing down, like a fist of wheat,
The unconscious emblem for the house's worth.

Conclusion surrounded it, and the accumulation
  After Lammas growth. Still coming on
Hart's-tongue by maiden-hair
  Thickened beneath the hedges, the corn levelled
And carried, long-since; but the earth
  (Its tint glowed in the house wall)
Out of the reddish dark still thrust up foison
  Through the browning-back of the exhausted year:

Thrust through the unweeded yard, where earth and house
  Debated the terrain. My eye
Caught in those flags a gravestone's fragment
  Set by a careful century. The washed inscription
Still keen, showed only a fragile stem
  A stave, a broken circlet, as
(Unintelligibly clear, craft in the sharp decrepitude)
  A pothook grooved its firm memorial.

Within, wet from the failing roof,
  Walls greened. Each hearth refitted
For a suburban whim, each room
  Denied what it was, diminished thus
To a barbarous mean, had comforted (but for a time)
  Its latest tenant. Angered, I turned to my path
Through the inhuman light, light that a fish might swim
  Stained by the greyness of the smoking fields.

Five centuries. And we? What we had not
  Made ugly, we had laid waste—
Left (I should say) the office to nature
  Whose blind battery, best fitted to perform it
Outdoes us, completes by persistence
  All that our negligence fails in. Saddened,
Yet angered beyond sadness, where the road
  Doubled upon itself I halted, for a moment
Facing the empty house and its laden barns.

CIVILITIES OF LAMPLIGHT

Without excess (no galaxies
Gauds, illiterate exclamations)
It betokens haven,
An ordering, the darkness held
But not dismissed. One man
Alone with his single light
Wading obscurity refines the instance,
Hollows the hedge-bound track, a sealed
Furrow on dark, closing behind him.

FIRE IN A DARK LANDSCAPE

And where it falls, a quality
Not of the night, but of the mind
As when, on the moonlit roofs,
A counterfeit snow
Whitely deceives us. And yet . . .
It is the meeting, of light
With dark, challenges the memory
To reveal itself, in an unfamiliar form,
As here: red branches
Into a transparency
In liquid motion, the winds'
Chimera of silk, twisting
Thickened with amber shadows,
A quality, not of the mind
But of fire on darkness.

THE RUIN

Dissolving, the coals shift. Rain swaddles us
  And the fire, driving its shadows through the room
Recalls us to our intention as the flames
  That, by turns, sink guttering or mount
To pour red light through every crater,
  Threaten the galleries of crumbling ash.

The ruins sag, then sift downwards,
  Their fall so soundless that, for the first time,
We distinguish the unbroken, muffled sibilance
  Rain has accompanied us with. Our talk
Recovers its theme—the ruin we should have visited
  Abandoned, now, in its own emptiness.

For the morning promised what, through the darkening air,
  Afternoon retracted, nor will the evening
Welcome us under its turmoil of wet leaves
  Where we have lost the keenness of such acridity
As a burnt ruin exhales long afterwards
  Into the coolness when rain has ceased.

It stands on the hill slope. Between green and green
  There is the boundary wall that circles
And now hides it. Within, one can see nothing
  Save the third, chequered indefinite green
Of treetops—until, skirting these limits
  One discovers, open upon the emptied confine, the gate.

For a week, the swift traffic of demolition
  That mottled with oil their stagnant rain,
Advanced through the deepening ruts,
  Converged on the house, disjointed, reassembled
And carted, flung (what had sprawled unhinged)
  The door into the wreckage and burnt both.

The door which, though elegant, leaned from the true
  A little to one side, was shamed
By the nearby, slender but rigid elm—
  An unchanging comedy, varied
Only as the seasons thought fit and as the days
  Under their shifting lights reviewed it.

The house was not ancient, but old: deserted,
  The slewed door had focused its rotting style
And, as proportion tugged from decrepitude
  A faint self-respect, it was the door
With the firmness of an aged but practised arbiter
  Bestowed it back over the entire ruin.

Impartial with imperfections, it could accuse
  By this scant presence its clustering neighbours
Gross with the poverty of utility. Thus challenging, it stayed,
  A problem for the authorities, a retreat for urchins
Until the urchins burnt half and the authorities
  Publicly accomplished what their ally had attempted by
    stealth.

There remains now the levelled parapet of earth,
  The bleak diagram of a foundation, a hearth
Focusing nothing and, cast into it, the filigree ghost
  Of an iron fanlight. Could we assemble
Beside its other fragments, that last grace
  Under this meaner roof, they would accuse us still—

And accusing, speak from beyond their dereliction
  Out of their life; as when a vase
Cracked into shards, would seem
  Baldly to confess, 'Men were here',
The arabesque reproves it, tracing in faint lines:
  'Ceremonies and order were here also.'

Nor could we answer: our houses
  Are no longer ourselves; they dare not
Enter our hopes as the guests of meditation
  To reanimate, warmed by this contact,
The laric world where the bowl glistens with presence
  Gracing the table on which it unfolds itself.

Thus fire, renewed at our hearth, consumes.
  Yet it cannot create from the squalor of moderation
A more than fortuitous glory, multiplying its image
  Over the projections of lacquered wood. Charged with their
    past,
Those relics smoulder before they are compounded
  And turned by the spade under a final neatness.

The window lightens. The shell parts
  Beyond between cloud and sky line.
Thunder-light, flushing the walls, yellows them
  Into a more ardent substance than their own
And can do no more. The effect is nature's
  Who ignores it, and in whose impoverishment we domicile.

STONE WALLS

At Chew Magna

In this unyielding, even
Afternoon glow
One by one
You could unfasten
Like the tendrils of ivy
The filaments of all these
Sagging networks
Where the shadowed space
Divides walls
Into friable pink blocks
And the glow would spread
More evenly over
Their resolved opacity,
But who would unmake
This dislocation where
Each is located?

AQUEDUCT

Let it stand
A stone guest
In an unhospitable land,
Its speech, the well's speech,
The unsealed source's,
Carrying thence
Its own sustenance. Its grace
Must be the match
Of the stream's strength,
And let the tone
Of the waters' flute
Brim with its gentle admonitions the conduit
stone.

ENCOUNTER

Birdless, the bush yet shakes
With a bird's alighting. Fate
Is transmitting flight
That rootwards flows,
Each unstilled spray
Tense like a dense arrival of targeted arrows.

From ANTECEDENTS

VI SOMETHING: A DIRECTION

Out of the shut cell of that solitude there is
  One egress, past point of interrogation.
Sun is, because it is not you; you are
  Since you are self, and self delimited
Regarding sun. It downs? I claim? Cannot
  Beyond such speech as this, gather conviction?
Judge, as you will, not what I say
  But what is, being said. It downs
Recovered, coverless, in a shriven light
  And you, returning, may to a shriven self
As from the scene, your self withdraws. You are downing
  Back from that autumn music of the light, which
Split by your need, to know the textures of your pain,
  Refuses them in your acceptance. You accept
An evening, washed of its overtones
  By strict seclusion, yet are not secluded
Withheld at your proper bounds. From there
  Your returns may enter, welcome strangers
Into a civil country (you were not the first
  To see it), but a country, natural and profuse
Unbroken by past incursions, as the theme
  Strung over stave, is rediscovered
After dismemberment in the canon, and over stave
  Can still proceed, unwound, unwinding

To its established presence, its territory
  Staked and sung; and the phrase descends
As a phase concluded. Released
  From knowing to acknowledgement, from prison
To powers, you are new-found
  Neighboured, having earned relation
With all that is other. Still you must wait,
  For evening's ashen, like the slow fire
Withdrawn through the whitened log
  Glinting through grain marks where the wood splits:
Let be its being: the scene extends
  Not hope, but the urgency that hopes for means.

THE CHURCHYARD WALL

Stone against stone, they are building back
  Round the steepled bulk, a wall
That enclosed from the neighbouring road
  The silent community of graves. James Bridle,
Jonathan Silk and Adam Bliss, you are well housed
  Dead, howsoever you lived—such headstones
Lettered and scrolled, and such a wall
  To repel the wind. The channel, first,
Dug to contain a base in solid earth
  And filled with the weightier fragments. The propped yews
Will scarcely outlast it; for, breached,
  It may be rebuilt. The graves weather
And the stone skulls, more ruinous
  Than art had made them, fade by their broken scrolls.
It protects the dead. The living regard it
  Once it is falling, and for the rest
Accept it. Again, the ivy
  Will clasp it down, save for the buried base
And that, where the frost has cracked,
  Must be trimmed, reset, and across its course
The barrier raised. Now they no longer
  Prepare: they build, judged by the dead.
The shales must fit, the skins of the wall-face
  Flush, but the rising stones

Sloped to the centre, balanced upon an incline.
  They work at ease, the shade drawn in
To the uncoped wall which casts it, unmindful
  For the moment, that they will be outlasted
By what they create, that their labour
  Must be undone. East and west
They cope it edgewise; to the south
  Where the talkers sit, taking its sun
When the sun has left it, they have lain
  The flat slabs that had fallen inwards
Mined by the ivy. They leave completed
  Their intent and useful labours to be ignored,
To pass into common life, a particle
  Of the unacknowledged sustenance of the eye,
Less serviceable than a house, but in a world of houses
  A merciful structure. The wall awaits decay.

WINTER-PIECE

You wake, all windows blind—embattled sprays
grained on the medieval glass.
Gates snap like gunshot
as you handle them. Five-barred fragility
sets flying fifteen rooks who go together
silently ravenous above this winter-piece
that will not feed them. They alight
beyond, scavenging, missing everything
but the bladed atmosphere, the white resistance.
Ruts with iron flanges track
through a hard decay
where you discern once more
oak-leaf by hawthorn, for the frost
rewhets their edges. In a perfect web
blanched along each spoke
and circle of its woven wheel,
the spider hangs, grasp unbroken
and death-masked in cold. Returning
you see the house glint-out behind
its holed and ragged glaze,
frost-fronds all streaming.

CANAL

Swans. I watch them
come unsteadying
the dusty, green
and curving arm
of water. Sinuously
both the live
bird and the bird
the water bends
into a white and wandering
reflection of itself,
go by in grace
a world of objects.
Symmetrically punched
now empty rivet-
holes betray
a sleeper fence:
below its raggedness
the waters darken
and above it rear
the saw-toothed houses
which the swinging
of the waters makes
scarcely less regular
in repetition. Swans
are backed by these, as
these are by
a sky of silhouettes,
all black and almost
all, indefinite.
A whitish smoke
in drifting diagonals
accents, divides
the predominance of street
and chimney lines,
where all is either
mathematically supine
or vertical, except
the pyramids of slag.
And, there, unseen
among such angularities—
a church, a black

freestanding witness
that a space of graves
invisibly is also
there. Only
its clock identifies
the tower between
the accompaniment of stacks
where everything
repeats itself—
the slag, the streets
and water that repeats
them all again
and spreads them rippling
out beneath
the eye of the discriminating
swans that seek
for something else
and the blank brink
concludes them without conclusion.

JOHN MAYDEW, *or* THE ALLOTMENT

Ranges
    of clinker heaps
        go orange now:
through cooler air
    an acrid drift
        seeps upwards
from the valley mills;
    the spoiled and staled
        distances invade
these closer comities
    of vegetable shade,
        glass-houses, rows
and trellises of red-
    ly flowering beans.
        This
is a paradise
    where you may smell
        the cinders

of quotidian hell beneath you;
      here grow
            their green reprieves
for those
      who labour, linger in
            their watch-chained waistcoats
rolled-back sleeves—
      the ineradicable
            peasant in the dispossessed
and half-tamed Englishman.
      By day, he makes
            a burrow of necessity
from which
      at evening, he emerges
            here.
A thoughtful yet unthinking man,
      John Maydew,
            memory stagnates
in you and breeds
      a bitterness; it grew
            and rooted in your silence
from the day
      you came
            unwitting out of war
in all the pride
      of ribbons and a scar
            to forty years
of mean amends . . .
      He squats
            within his shadow
and a toad
      that takes
            into a slack and twitching jaw
the worms he proffers it,
      looks up at him
            through eyes that are
as dimly faithless
      as the going years.
            For, once returned
he found that he
      must choose between
            an England, profitlessly green

and this—
        a seamed and lunar grey
                where slag in lavafolds
unrolls beneath him.
        The valley gazes up
                through kindling eyes
as, unregarded at his back
        its hollows deepen
                with the black, extending shadows
and the sounds of day
        explore its coming cavities,
                the night's
refreshed recesses.
        Tomorrow
                he must feed its will,
his interrupted pastoral
        take heart into
                those close
and gritty certainties that lie
        a glowing ruse
                all washed in hesitations now.
He eyes the toad
        beating
                in the assuagement
of his truce.

STEEL

The night shift

Slung from the gantries cranes
patrol in air and parry
lights the furnaces fling up at them.
Clamour is deepest in the den beneath,
fire fiercest at the frontier where
an arm of water doubles
and disjoints it. There is a principle, a pulse
in all these molten and metallic contraries,
this sweat unseen. For men
facelessly habituated to the glare

outstare it, guide the girders
from their high and iron balconies
and keep the simmering slag-trucks
feeding heap on heap
in regular, successive, sea-on-shore
concussive bursts of dry
and falling sound. And time
is all this measured voice would seem
to ask, until it uncreate
the height and fabric of the light-
lunged, restive, flame-eroded night.

CROW

The inspecting eye
shows cold
amid the head's
disquieted iridescence.
The whole bird sits
rocking at a vantage
clumsily. The glance
alone is steady
and a will behind it
rights the stance,
corrects all disposition
to ungainly action.
Acting, it will be
as faultless as its eye
in a concerted drop
on carrion; or watch
it fly—the insolence
transfers to wing-tip
and the action wears
an ease that's merciless,
all black assumption,
mounting litheness.
The blown bird,
inaccessible its intimations
of the wind, 'Stay
where you are' is

what it says and we
poor swimmers
in that element
stay, to bear
with clumsy eye
affronted witness at its ways in air.

THE HAND AT CALLOW HILL FARM

Silence. The man defined
The quality, ate at his separate table
Silent, not because silence was enjoined
But was his nature. It shut him round
Even at outdoor tasks, his speech
Following upon a pause, as though
A hesitance to comply had checked it—
Yet comply he did, and willingly:
Pause and silence: both
Were essential graces, a reticence
Of the blood, whose calm concealed
The tutelary of that upland field.

THE PICTURE OF J.T. IN A PROSPECT OF STONE

What should one
    wish a child
        and that, one's own
emerging
    from between
        the stone lips
of a sheep-stile
    that divides
        village graves

and village green?
—Wish her
the constancy of stone.
—But stone
is hard.
—Say, rather
it resists
the slow corrosives
and the flight
of time
and yet it takes
the play, the fluency
from light.
—How would you know
the gift you'd give
was the gift
she'd wish to have?
—Gift is giving,
gift is meaning:
first
I'd give
then let her
live with it
to prove
its quality the better and
thus learn
to love
what (to begin with)
she might spurn.
—You'd
moralize a gift?
—I'd have her
understand
the gift I gave her.
—And so she shall
but let her play
her innocence away
emerging
as she does
between
her doom (unknown),
her unmown green.

THE CHESTNUT AVENUE

At Alton House

Beneath their flames, cities of candelabra
  Gathering-in a more than civic dark
Sway between green and gloom,
  Prepare a way of hushed submergence
Where the eye descries no human house,
  But a green trajectory in whose depths
Glimmers a barrier of stone. At the wind's invasion
  The greenness teeters till the indented parallels
Lunge to a restive halt, defying still
  The patient geometry that planted them
Thus, in their swaying stations. We have lent them
  Order—they, greeting that gift
  With these incalculable returns. Mindless
  They lead the mind its ways, deny
The imposition of its frontiers, as the wind, their ally,
  Assails the civility of the façade they hide
Their green indifference barbarous at its panes.

FOUR KANTIAN LYRICS

for Paul Roubiczek

1 *On a Theme of Pasternak*

I stared, but not to seize
the point of things: it was an incidental
sharpness held me there,
watching a sea of leaves
put out the sun. Spark
by spark, they drew it slowly down
sifting the hoard in glints
and pinheads. Rents of space
threatened to let it through
but, no—at once, the same
necessity that tamed the sky

to a single burning tone
would drag it deeper. Light
was suddenly beneath the mass
and silhouette of skirts and fringes,
shrinking to a glow on grass.
With dark, a breeze comes in
sends staggering the branches'
blackened ledges till they rear
recoiling. And now the trees are there
no longer, one can hear it climb
repeatedly their sullen hill
of leaves, rake and rouse them,
then their gathered tide
set floating all the house on air.

2 *What it was like*

It was like the approach of flame
treading the tinder, a fleet
cascade of it taking tree-toll,
halting below the hill and then
covering the corn-field's dryness
in an effortless crescendo. One heard
in the pause of the receding silence
the whole house grow
tense through its ties, the beams
brace beneath pantiles
for the coming burst. It came
and went. The blinded pane
emerged from the rainsheet
to an after-water world,
its green confusion brought
closer greener. The baptism
of the shining house was done
and it was like the calm
a church aisle harbours
tasting of incense, space and stone.

3 *An Insufficiency of Earth*

The wind goes over it. You see
the broken leaf-cope breathe
subsidingly, and lift itself
like water levelling. Stemmed,
this cloud of green, this mammoth
full of detail shifts
its shimmering, archaic head
no more. You think it for a second
hugely dead, until the ripple
soundless on the further corn,
is roaring in it. We cannot pitch
our paradise in such a changeful
nameless place and our encounters
with it. An insufficiency of earth
denies our constancy. For,
content with the iridescence of the moment,
we must flow with the wood-fleece
in a war of forms, the wind
gone over us, and we
drinking its imprints, faceless as the sea.

4 *How it happened*

It happened like this: I heard
from the farm beyond, a grounded
churn go down. The sound
chimed for the wedding of the mind
with what one could not see,
the further fields, the seamless
spread of space, and then,
all bestial ease, the cows
foregathered by the milking place
in a placid stupor. There are two
ways to marry with a land—
first, this bland and blind
submergence of the self, an act
of kind and questionless. The other
is the thing I mean, a whole
event, a happening, the sound
that brings all space in
for its bound, when self is clear

as what we keenest see and hear:
no absolute of eye can tell
the utmost, but the glance
goes shafted from us like a well.

UP AT LA SERRA

The shadow
    ran before it lengthening
        and a wave went over.
Distance
    did not obscure
        the machine of nature:
you could watch it
    squander and recompose itself
        all day, the shadow-run
the sway of the necessity down there
    at the cliff-base
        crushing white from blue.
Come in
    by the arch
        under the campanile parrocchiale
and the exasperation of the water
    followed you,
        its *Soldi, soldi*
unpicking the hill-top peace
    insistently.
        He knew, at twenty
all the deprivations such a place
    stored for the man
        who had no more to offer
than a sheaf of verse
    in the style of Quasimodo.
        Came the moment,
he would tell it
    in a poem
        without rancour, a lucid
testament above his name
    Paolo
        Bertolani

—Ciao, Paolo!
        —Ciao
                Giorgino!
He would put them
        all in it—
                Giorgino going
over the hill
        to look for labour;
                the grinder
of knives and scissors
        waiting to come up, until
                someone would hoist his wheel
on to a back, already
        hooped to take it,
                so you thought
the weight must crack
        the curvature. And then:
                Beppino and Beppino
friends
        who had in common
                nothing except their names and friendship;
and the sister of the one
        who played the accordion
                and under all
the *Soldi, soldi,*
        sacra conversazione
                del mare—
della madre.
        Sometimes
                the men had an air of stupefaction:
La Madre:
        it was the women there
                won in a truceless enmity.
At home
        a sepia-green
                Madonna di Foligno
shared the wall
        with the October calendar—
                Lenin looked out of it,
Mao
        blessing the tractors
                and you told

the visitors:
We are not communists
although we call ourselves communists
we are what you English
would call . . . socialists.
He believed
that God was a hypothesis,
that the party would bring in
a synthesis, that he
would edit the local paper for them,
or perhaps
go northward to Milan;
or would he grow
as the others had—son
to the puttana-madonna
in the curse,
chafed by the maternal knot and by
the dream of faithlessness,
uncalloused hands,
lace, white
at the windows of the sailors' brothels
in the port five miles away?
Soldi—
soldi—
some
worked at the naval yards
and some, like him
were left between
the time the olives turned
from green to black
and the harvest of the grapes,
idle
except for hacking wood.
Those
with an acre of good land
had vines, had wine
and self-respect. Some
carried down crickets
to the garden of the mad Englishwoman
who could
not
tolerate

crickets, and they received
    soldi, soldi
        for recapturing them . . .
The construction
    continued as heretofore
        on the villa of the Milanese dentist
as the evening
    came in with news:
        —*We have won*
the election.
    —*At the café*
        the red flag is up.
He turned back
    quickly beneath the tower.
        Giorgino
who wanted to be a waiter
    wanted to be commissar
        piling *sassi*
into the dentist's wall.
    Even the harlot's mother
        who had not dared
come forth because her daughter
    had erred in giving birth,
        appeared by the *Trattoria della Pace.*
She did not enter
    the masculine precinct,
        listening there, her shadow
lengthened-out behind her
    black as the uniform of age
        she wore
on back and head.
    This was the Day
        which began all reckonings
she heard them say
    with a woman's ears;
        she liked
the music from the wireless.
    The padre
        pulled
at his unheeded angelus
    and the Day went down behind
        the town in the bay below

where—come the season—
they would be preparing
with striped umbrellas,
for the *stranieri* and *milanesi*—
treason so readily compounded
by the promiscuous stir
on the iridescent sliding water.
He had sought
the clear air of the cliff.
—Salve, Giorgino
—Salve
Paolo, have you
heard
that we have won the election?
—I am writing
a poem about it:
it will begin
here, with the cliff and with the sea
following its morning shadow in.

RHENISH WINTER

A montage after Apollinaire

In the house
of the vine-grower
women were sewing
Lenchen
pile up the stove
put on
water for the coffee
—Now that the cat
has thawed itself
it stretches-out flat
—Bans are in
at last for Gertrude
and Martin her neighbour
The blind nightingale
essayed a song

but quailed in its cage
as the screech-owl wailed
The cypress out there
has the air of the pope
setting out in snow
—That's the post
has stopped for a chat
with the new schoolmaster
—This winter is bitter
the wine
will taste all the better
—The sexton
the deaf and lame one
is dying
—The daughter
of the old burgomaster
is working
a stole in embroidery
for the priest's birthday
Out there
thanks to the wind
the forest gave forth
with its grave organ voice
Dreamy Herr Traum
turned up with his sister
Frau Sorge
unexpectedly
Mended
you call these
stockings mended Käthe
Bring
the coffee the butter the spread
bread in Set
the jam and the lard and
don't forget milk
—Lenchen
a little more
of that coffee please
—You could imagine
that what the wind says
was in Latin
—A little more

Lenchen
  —Are you sad
    Lotte my dear
I think
  she's sweet on somebody
    —God
keep her clear
  of that—As for me
    I love nobody
but myself—Gently
  gently
    grandmother's telling her rosary
—I need
  sugar candy
    I've a cough Leni
—There's Paul
  off with his ferret
    hunting for rabbits
The wind
  blew on the firs
    till they danced in a ring
Love makes
  a poor thing of Lotte
    Ilse
isn't life bright
  In the snarled stems
    the night
was turning the vineyards
  to charnels of snow
    shrouds
lay there unfolded
  curs
    bayed at cold travellers
He's dead
  listen
    from the church
the low bell-tone
  The sexton had gone
    Lise

c

the stove's dwindled to nothing
rekindle it
The women
made the sign of the cross
and the night
abolished their outline.

LE MUSÉE IMAGINAIRE

An Aztec sacrifice,
beside the head of Pope:
eclectic and unresolvable.
We admire the first
for its expressiveness, the second
because we understand it—
can re-create
its circumstances, and share
(if not the presuppositions)
the aura
of the civilities surrounding it.
The other, in point
at any rate, of violence
touches us more nearly.
and yet . . . it is cruel
but unaccountably so; for the temper of awe
demanded by the occasion, escapes us:
it is not
better than we are—
it is merely different.
Expressive, certainly. But of what?
Our loss is absolute, yet unfelt
because inexact. The head
of Alexander Pope,
stiller, attests the more tragic lack
by remaining
what it was meant to be;
intelligible,
it forbids us to approach it.

AT WELLS

Polyphony

The unmoving vault
    receives their movement
        voices
falling flights
    niched
        on the sudden, providential hand
of air
    daring to reassume
        the height that
spanned and hemmed un-
    til (like light
        entering amber)
they take and hold it
    and their time
        its space
sustain
    in a single element the chord of grace.

SEA POEM

A whiter bone:
    the sea-voice
        in a multiple monody
crowding towards that end.
    It is as if
        the transparencies of sound
composing such whiteness
    disposed many layers
        with a sole movement
of the various surface,
    the depths, bottle-glass green
        the bed, swaying
like a fault in the atmosphere, each
    shift
        with its separate whisper, each whisper

a breath of that singleness
that 'moves together
if it moves at all',
and its movement is ceaseless,
and to one end—
the grinding
a whiter bone.

HEAD HEWN WITH AN AXE

The whittled crystal: fissured
For the invasion of shadows.

The stone book, its
Hacked leaves
Frozen in granite.

The meteorite, anatomized
By the geometer. And to what end?
To the enrichment of the alignment:
Sun against shade against sun:
That daily food, which
Were it not for such importunities
Would go untasted:

The suave block, desecrated
In six strokes. The light
Is staunching its wounds.

THE GOSSAMERS

Autumn. A haze is gold
By definition. This one lit
The thread of gossamers
That webbed across it
Out of shadow and again
Through rocking spaces which the sun

Claimed in the leafage. Now
I saw for what they were
These glitterings in grass, on air,
Of certainties that ride and plot
The currents in their tenuous stride
And, as they flow, must touch
Each blade and, touching, know
Its green resistance. Undefined
The haze of autumn in the mind
Is gold, is glaze.

CLOUD CHANGE

First light—call it
First doubt among shadows
As the seam splits
At sky-level. The dark
Scarcely disperses.
The partial light
Drifts into it from beneath,
Flushes the atmosphere
Transparent. Call it
Dismissal, elemental
Reprimand to reluctance:
The dark is losing
In the day-long sway
That neither can win. Call it—
Defeat into dialogue.

LETTER FROM COSTA BRAVA

Its crisp sheets, unfolded,
Give on to a grove, where
Citrons conduct the eye
Past the gloom of foliage
Towards the glow of stone. They write

Of a mesmeric clarity
In the fissures of those walls
And of the unseizable lizards, jewelled
Upon them. But let them envy
What they cannot see:
This sodden, variable green
Igniting against the grey.

OVER BROOKLYN BRIDGE

Mayakovsky
    has it!—
        'in the place
of style, an austere
    disposition of bolts.'
        The poet cedes
his elocutionary function
    to the telephone book:
        Helmann
Salinas
    Yarmolinsky,
        words
reciprocally
    kindling one another
        like the train of fire
over a jewel box.
    Miss Moore
        had a negress
for a maid whose father
    was a Cherokee.
        'No', she said
'I do not live in town
    I live in Brooklyn.
        I was afraid
you wouldn't like it here—
    it's gotten so ugly.'
        I liked Brooklyn
with its survival
    of wooden houses
        and behind trees

the balconies colonnaded.
    And what I liked
        about the bridge
was the uncertainty
    the way
        the naked steel
would not go naked
    but must wear
        its piers of stone—
as the book says
    'stylistically
        its weakest feature.'
I like
    such weaknesses, the pull
        the stone base
gives to the armature.
    I live
        in a place of stone
if it's still there
    by the time I've sailed to it.
        Goodbye
Miss Moore
    I hope
        the peacock's feather you once saw
at the house of Ruskin
    has kept its variegations.
        Jewels
have histories:
    'I never did
        care for Mallarmé'
she said
    and the words
        in the book of names
are flames not bolts.

ODE TO ARNOLD SCHOENBERG

on a performance of his concerto for violin

At its margin
the river's double willow
that the wind
variously
disrupts, effaces
and then restores
in shivering planes:
it is
calm morning.
The twelve notes
(from the single root
the double tree)
and their reflection:
let there be
unity—this,
however the winds rout
or the wave disperses
remains, as
in the liberation of the dissonance
beauty would seem discredited
and yet is not:
redefined
it may be reachieved,
thus to proceed
through discontinuities
to the whole in which
discontinuities are held
like the foam in chalcedony
the stone, enriched
by the tones' impurity.
The swayed mirror
half-dissolves
and the reflection
yields to reflected light.
Day. The bell-clang
goes down the air
and, like a glance
grasping upon its single thread
a disparate scene,

crosses and re-creates
the audible morning.
All meet at cockcrow
when our common sounds
confirm our common bonds.
Meshed in meaning
by what is natural
we are discontented
for what is more,
until the thread
of an instrument pursue
a more than common meaning.
But to redeem
both the idiom and the instrument
was reserved
to this exiled Jew—to bring
by fiat
certainty from possibility.
For what is sound
made reintelligible
but the unfolded word
branched and budded,
the wintered tree
creating, cradling space
and then
filling it with verdure?

FACE AND IMAGE

Between
the image of it
and your face: Between
is the unchartable country,
variable, virgin
terror and territory.

The image—
that most desperate act
of portraiture—
I carry and my mind
marries it willingly,
though the forfeiture's
foreknown already: admit
the reality and you see
the distance from it.

The face—
mouth, eyes and forehead,
substantial things,
advance their frontier
clear against all imaginings:

And yet—
seeing a face, what
do we see?
It is not
the one
incontrovertible you or me.

For, still, we must
in all the trust of seeing
trace
the face in the image, image in the face.

To love
is to see,
to let be
this disparateness
and to live within
the unrestricted boundary between.

Even an uncherished face
forces us
to acknowledge
its distinctness, its continuance thus;
then how should these
lips not compound the theme
and being of all appearances?

THE SNOW FENCES

They are fencing the upland against
the drifts this wind, those clouds
would bury it under: brow and bone
know already that levelling zero
as you go, an aching skeleton,
in the breathtaking rareness of winter air.

Walking here, what do you see?
Little more, through wind-teased eyes,
than a black, iron tree
and, there, another, a straggle
of low and broken wall between, grass
sapped of its greenness, day going.

The farms are few: spread
as wide, perhaps, as when
the Saxons who found them, chose
these airy and woodless spaces
and froze here before they fed
the unsuperseded burial ground.

Ahead, the church's dead-white
limewash will dazzle the mind
as, dazed, you enter to escape:
despite the stillness here, the chill
of wash-light scarcely seems
less penetrant than the hill-top wind.

Between the graves, you find
a beheaded pigeon, the blood and grain
trailed from its bitten crop, as alien to all
the day's pallor as the raw
wounds of the earth, turned above
a fresh solitary burial.

A plaque of staining metal
distinguishes this grave among
an anonymity whose stones
the frosts have scaled, thrusting under
as if they grudged the ground
its ill-kept memorials.

The bitter darkness drives you
back valleywards, and again you bend
joint and tendon to encounter
the wind's force and leave behind
the nameless stones, the snow-shrouds
of a waste season: they are fencing
the upland against those years, those clouds.

WIND

Insistence being of its nature,
thus a refusal to insist is to meet it
on equal terms. For one is neither
bull to bellow with it, nor barometer
to slide, accommodated, into the mood's trough
once the thing has departed. The woods
shook, as though it were the day
of wrath that furrowed its sentence
in the rippled forms, the bleached
obliquity of the winter grass.
Black branches were staggering
and climbing the air, rattling
on one another like a hailfall:
they clawed and tapped, as if the whole
blind company of the dead
bound in its lime, had risen
to repossess this ground. As if—
but time was in mid-career
streaming through space: the dead
were lying in customary quiet.
Kin to the sole bird abroad
gone tinily over like a flung stone,
one hung there against the wind,
blown to a judgment, yes, brought
to bear fronting the airs' commotion.
The noise above, and the rooted silence
under it, poised one in place,
and time said: 'I rescind
the centuries with now,' and space
banishing one from there to here:
'You are not God. You are not the wind.'

THE DOOR

Too little
has been said
of the door, its one
face turned to the night's
downpour and its other
to the shift and glisten of firelight.

Air, clasped
by this cover
into the room's book,
is filled by the turning
pages of dark and fire
as the wind shoulders the panels, or unsteadies that burning.

Not only
the storm's
breakwater, but the sudden
frontier to our concurrences, appearances,
and as full of the offer of space
as the view through a cromlech is.

For doors
are both frame and monument
to our spent time,
and too little
has been said
of our coming through and leaving by them.

THE WEATHERCOCKS

Bitten and burned into mirrors of thin gold,
the weathercocks, blind from the weather,
have their days of seeing as they
grind round on their swivels.

A consciousness of pure metal
begins to melt when (say)
that light 'which never was'
begins to be

And catches the snow's accents
in each dip and lap, and the wide
stains on the thawed ploughland are like continents
across a rumpled map.

Their gold eyes hurt
at the corduroy lines come clear whose grain
feels its way over the shapes of the rises
joining one brown accord of stain and stain.

And the patterning stretches, flown
out on a wing of afternoon cloud that the sun
is changing to sea-wet sandflats,
hummocked in tiny dunes like the snow half-gone—

As if the sole wish of the light
were to harrow with mind matter, to shock
wide the glance of the tree-knots and the stone-eyes
the sun is bathing, to waken the weathercocks.

A GIVEN GRACE

Two cups,
a given grace,
afloat and white
on the mahogany pool
of table. They unclench
the mind, filling it
with themselves.
Though common ware,
these rare reflections,
coolness of brown
so strengthens and refines
the burning of their white,

you would not wish
them other than they are—
you, who are challenged
and replenished by
those empty vessels.

SAVING THE APPEARANCES

The horse is white. Or it
appears to be under this
November light that could
well be October. It goes
as nimbly as a spider does
but it is gainly: the great
field makes it small
so that it seems
to crawl out of the distance
and to grow not larger
but less slow. Stains
on its sides show where
the mud is and the power
now overmasters the fragility
of its earlier bearing. Tall
it shudders over one and bends
a full neck, cropping
the foreground, blotting
the whole space back
behind those pounding feet.
Mounted, one feels the sky
as much the measure of the event
as the field had been, and all
the divisions of the indivisible
unite again, or seem
to do as when the approaching
horse was white, on this
November unsombre day
where what appears, is.

From IN WINTER WOODS

III NOCTURNAL

Shade confounds shadow now. Blue
is the last tone left
in a wide view
dimming in shrinking vista.
Birds, crossing it,
lose themselves rapidly
behind coverts where all the lines
are tangled, the tangles
hung with a halo of cold dew.
The sun smearily edges
out of the west, and a moon
risen already, will soon
take up to tell in its own style
this tale of confusions:
that light which seemed
to have drawn out after it
all space, melting in horizontals,
must yield now
to a new, tall beam,
a single, judicious eye: it will have
roof behind roof once more, and these
shadows of buildings
must be blocked-in
and ruled with black, and shadows
of black iron must flow
beneath the wrought-iron trees.

THE CAVERN

Obliterate
mythology as you unwind
this mountain-interior
into the negative-dark mind,
as there
the gypsum's snow

the limestone stair
and boneyard landscape grow
into the identity of flesh.

Pulse of the water-drop,
veils and scales, fins
and flakes of the forming
leprous rock,
how should these
inhuman, turn
human with such chill affinities?

Hard to the hand,
these mosses not of moss,
but nostrils, pits
of eyes, faces
in flight and prints
of feet where no feet ever were,
elude the mind's
hollow that would contain
this canyon within a mountain.

Not far
enough from the familiar,
press
in under a deeper dark until
the curtained sex
the arch, the streaming buttress
have become
the self's unnameable and shaping home.

ARIZONA DESERT

Eye
drinks the dry orange ground,
the cowskull
bound to it by shade:
sun-warped, the layers
of flaked and broken bone
unclench into petals,
into eyelids of limestone:

Blind glitter
that sees
spaces and steppes expand
of the purgatories possible
to us and
impossible.

Upended trees
in the Hopi's desert orchard
betoken
unceasing unspoken war,
return
the levelling light,
imageless arbiter.

A dead snake
pulsates again
as, hidden, the beetles' hunger
mines through the tunnel of its drying skin.

Here, to be,
is to sound
patience deviously
and follow
like the irregular corn
the water underground.

Villages
from mud and stone
parch back
to the dust they humanize
and mean
marriage, a loving lease
on sand, sun, rock and
Hopi
means peace.

A DEATH IN THE DESERT

in memory of Homer Vance

There are no crosses
on the Hopi graves. They lie
shallowly
under a scattering
of small boulders. The sky
over the desert
with its sand-grain stars
and the immense equality
between
desert and desert sky,
seem
a scope and ritual
enough to stem
death and to be its equal.

'Homer
is the name,' said
the old Hopi doll-maker.
I met him in summer. He was dead
when I came back that autumn.

He had sat
like an Olympian
in his cool room
on the rock-roof of the world,
beyond the snatch
of circumstance
and was to die
beating a burro out of his corn-patch.

'That',
said his neighbour
'was a week ago.' And the week
that lay
uncrossably between us
stretched into sand,

into the spread
of the endless
waterless sea-bed beneath
whose space outpacing sight
receded as speechless and as wide as death.

ON THE MOUNTAIN

Nobody there:
no body,
thin aromatic air
pricking the wide nostrils
that inhale the dark.

Blank brow freezing
where the blaze of snow
carries beyond the summit
up over a satin cloud meadow
to confront the moon.

Nobody sees
the snow-free tree-line,
the aspens weightlessly shivering
and the surrounding pine
that, hardly
lifting their heavy
pagodas of leaves,
yet make a continuous
sound as of sea-wash
around the mountain lake.

And nobody climbs
the dry collapsing ledges
down to the place
to stand
in solitary, sharpened reflection
save for that swaying moon-face.

Somebody
finding nobody there
found gold also:
gold gone, he
(stark in his own redundancy)
must needs go too
and here, sun-warped
and riddled by moon, decays
his house which nobody occupies.

LAS TRAMPAS U.S.A.

for Robert and Priscilla Bunker

I go through hollyhocks
in a dry garden, up
to the house,
knock, then ask
in English for the key
to Las Trampas church.
The old woman
says in Spanish: I
do not speak English
so I say: Where
is the church key
in Spanish.
—You see those
three men working: you
ask them. She
goes in, I
go on
preparing to ask
them in Spanish:
Hi, they say
in American. Hello
I say and ask
them in English
where is the key
to the church and they
say: He has it
gesturing to a fourth

man working
hoeing a corn-field
nearby, and to him
(in Spanish): Where is
the church key? And he:
I have it.—O.K.
they say in
Spanish-American:
You bring it (and
to me in English)
He'll bring it. You
wait for him
by the church door.
Thank you, I say and they
reply in American
You're welcome. I go
once more and
await in shadow
the key: he
who brings it is not
he of the hoe, but
one of the three
men working, who
with a Castilian grace
ushers me in
to this place
of coolness out
of the August sun.

MR. BRODSKY

I had heard
before, of an
American who would have preferred
to be an Indian;
but not
until Mr. Brodsky, of one
whose professed and long
pondered-on passion
was to become a Scot,

who even sent for haggis and oatcakes
across continent.
Having read him
in Cambridge English
a verse or two
from MacDiarmid,
I was invited
to repeat the reading
before a Burns Night Gathering
where the Balmoral Pipers
of Albuquerque would
play in the haggis
out of its New York tin.
Of course, I said
No. No. I could *not* go
and then
half-regretted I had not been.
But to console
and cure the wish, came
Mr. Brodsky, bringing
his pipes and played
until the immense, distended
bladder of leather seemed
it could barely contain its water—
tears (idle
tears) for the bridal of Annie Laurie
and Morton J. Brodsky.
A bagpipe in a dwelling is
a resonant instrument
and there he stood
lost in the gorse
the heather or whatever
six thousand
miles and more
from the infection's source,
in our neo-New Mexican parlour
where I had heard
before of an
American who would have preferred
to be merely an Indian.

AT BARSTOW

Nervy with neons, the main drag
was all there was. A placeless place.
A faint flavour of Mexico in the tacos
tasting of gasoline. Trucks refuelled
before taking off through space. Someone lived
in the houses with their houseyards wired
like tiny Belsens. The Götterdämmerung
would be like this. No funeral pyres, no choirs
of lost trombones. An Untergang
without a clang, without
a glimmer of gone glory
however dimmed. At the motel desk
was a photograph of Roy Rogers
signed. It was here
he made a stay. He did not
ride away on Trigger
through the high night, the tilted
Pleiades overhead, the polestar low, no
going off until
the eyes of beer-cans
had ceased to glint at him
and the desert darknesses
had quenched the neons. He was spent.
He was content. Down he lay.
The passing trucks patrolled his sleep,
the shifted gears contrived
a muffled fugue against the fading of his day
and his dustless, undishonoured stetson rode
beside the bed,
glowed in the pulsating, never-final twilight
there, at that execrable conjunction
of gasoline and desert air.

UTE MOUNTAIN

'When I am gone'
the old chief said
'if you need me, call me',
and down he lay, became stone.

They were giants then
(as you may see),
and we
are not the shadows of such men.

The long splayed Indian hair
spread ravelling out
behind the rocky head
in groins, ravines;

petered across the desert plain
through Colorado,
transmitting force
in a single undulant unbroken line

from toe to hair-tip: there
profiled, inclined away from one
are features, foreshortened, and the high
blade of the cheekbone.

Reading it so, the eye
can take the entire great
straddle of mountain-mass,
passing down elbows, knees and feet.

'If you need me, call me.'
His singularity dominates the plain
as we call to our aid his image:
thus men make a mountain.

IN CONNECTICUT

White, these villages. White
their churches without altars. The first snow
falls through a grey-white sky
and birch-twig whiteness turns
whiter against the grey. White
the row of pillars (each
of them is a single tree), the walls
sculptureless. 'This church was gathered
in 1741. In 1742
by act of the General Assembly of Connecticut
this territory was incorporated
and was named Judea.'
The sun passes, the elms
enter as lace shadows, then
go out again. White . . .
'Our minister is fine. He's a minister
in church, and a man outside.'—delivered
with the same shadowless conviction
as her invitation, when
lowering, leaning
out of the window she was cleaning
she had said: 'Our doors
are always open.'

MAINE WINTER

Ravenous the flock
who with an artist's
tact, dispose
their crow-blue-black
over the spread of snow—

Trackless, save where
by stalled degrees
a fox flaringly goes
with more of the hunter's caution than
of the hunter's ease.

The flock
have sighted him, are his match
and more, with their artist's eye
and a score of beaks against
a fox, paws clogged, and a single pair of jaws.

And they mass to the red-on-white
conclusion, sweep
down between
a foreground all snow-scene and a distance
all cliff-tearing seascape.

IN LONGFELLOW'S LIBRARY

Sappho
and the Venus de Milo
gaze out past
the scintillations from
the central
candelabrum
to where
(on an upper shelf)
plaster Goethe
in a laurel
crown, looks
down divided
from a group
dancing a
tarantella, by
the turquoise butterfly
that Agassiz
brought back
dead: below
these, the busts of
Homer, Aeschylus
and Sophocles still
pedestalled where
they ambushed Hiawatha.

ON ELEVENTH STREET

A mosaicist of minute
attentions composed it,
arranged the gravel
walks, where there is not
room for any, and the neat
hedges of privet: the complete
Second Cemetery
of the Spanish and Portuguese
Synagogue, Shearith
Israel, in the City of
New York
eighteen-five to
twenty-nine, could be
cut out, and carried
away by three
men, one at each
corner: a tight
triangle between two
building ends, the third
side a wall, white-washed
topped by a railing, and a gate
in it on to the street.

A GARLAND FOR THOMAS EAKINS

I

He lived
from his second year
at seventeen twentynine
Mount Vernon Street
Philadelphia
Pennsylvania where
he painted his
father and his sisters

and he died
in Pennsylvania in
Philadelphia at
seventeen twentynine
Mount Vernon Street.

II

Anatomy, perspective
and reflection: a boat
in three inclinations:
to the wind, to the waves
and to the picture-frame.
Those are the problems. What
does a body propose
that a boat does not?

III

Posing the model
for 'The Concert Singer' he
stood her
relative to a grid
placed vertically
behind her. There was a spot
before her
on the wall that
she must look at.
To her dress
by the intersections
of the grid he tied
coloured ribbons, thus
projecting her
like an architect's elevation
on a plane
that was vertical, the canvas
at a right angle
to the eye and perpendicular
to the floor.
What does the man
who sees
trust to
if not the eye? He trusts
to knowledge
to right appearances.

IV

—And what do you think of
that, Mr. Eakins? (A Whistler)
—I think that that
is a very cowardly way to paint.

V

A fat woman
by Rubens
is not a fat
woman but a fiction.

VI

The Eakins portrait
(said Whitman)
sets me down
in correct style
without feathers.
And when they
said to him:
Has Mr. Eakins no
social gifts? he said
to them: What are
'social gifts'?—
The parlour puts
quite its own
measure upon social gifts.

VII

The figures of perception
as against
the figures of elocution.
What they wanted
was to be Medici
in Philadelphia
and they survive
as Philadelphians.

VIII

The accord with that
which asked
only to be recorded:
'How beautiful,' he said,
'an old lady's skin is:
all those wrinkles!'

IX

Only
to be recorded!
and his stare
in the self-portrait
calculates the abyss
in the proposition. He dies
unsatisfied, born
to the stubborn
anguish of
those eyes.

THE WELL

in a Mexican convent

Leaning on
the parapet stone
Listening down
the long, dark
sheath through which the standing
shaft of water
sends its echoings up
Catching, as it stirs
the steady seethings
that mount and mingle
with surrounding sounds
from the neighbouring
barrack-yard: soldiery
—heirs, no doubt
of the gunnery that gashed
these walls of tattered

frescoes, the bullet-
holes now socketed
deeper by sunlight
and the bright gaps
giving on to the square
and there revealing
strollers in khaki
with their girls Aware
of a well-like
cool throughout
the entire, clear
sunlit ruin,
of the brilliant cupids
above the cistern
that hold up
a baldachin of stone
which is not there
Hearing the tide
of insurrection
subside through time
under the still-
painted slogans
Hemos servido
lealmente
la revolución

ON A MEXICAN STRAW CHRIST

This is not the event. This
Is a man of straw,
The legs straw-thin
The straw-arms shent
And nailed. And yet this dry
Essence of agony must be
Close-grained to the one
They lifted down, when
Consummatum est the event was done.
Below the baroque straw-
Haloed basket-head
And the crown, far more

Like a cap, woven
For a matador than a crown of thorn,
A gap recedes: it makes
A mouth-in-pain, the teeth
Within its sideways-slashed
And gritted grin, are
Verticals of straw, and they
Emerge where the mask's
Chin ceases and become
Parallels plunging down, their sum
The body of God. Beneath,
Two feet join in one
Cramped culmination, as if
To say: 'I am the un-
Resurrection and the Death.'

WEEPER IN JALISCO

A circle of saints, all
hacked, mauled, bound,
bleed in a wooden frieze
under the gloom of the central
dome of gold. They
are in paradise now
and we are not—
baroque feet gone
funnelling up, a blood-
bought, early resurrection
leaving us this
tableau of wounds, the crack
in the universe sealed
behind their flying backs.
We are here, and a woman
sprawls and wails to them
there, the gold screen
glistening, hemming her
under, till her keening
fills the stone ear
of the whole, hollow sanctum
and she is the voice

those wounds cry through
unappeasably bleeding where
her prone back shoulders
the price and weight
of forfeited paradise.

IDYLL

Washington Square, San Francisco

A door:
    PER L'UNIVERSO
        is what it says
above it.
    You must approach
        more nearly
(the statue
    of Benjamin Franklin watching you)
        before you see
La Gloria di Colui
    che tutto muove
        PER L'UNIVERSO
—leaning
    along the lintel—
        penetra e risplende
across this church
    for Italian Catholics:
        Dante
unscrolling in rhapsody.
    Cool
        the January sun,
that with an intensity
    the presence of the sea
        makes more exact,
chisels the verse with shade
    and lays
        on the grass
a deep and even
    Californian green,
        while a brilliance

throughout the square
        flatters the meanness of its architecture.
                Beyond
there is the flood
        which skirts this pond
                and tugs the ear
towards it: cars
        thick on the gradients of the city
                shift sun and sound—
a constant ground-bass
        to these provincialisms of the piazza
                tasting still
of Lerici and Genova.
        Here
                as there
the old men sit
        in a mingled odour
                of cheroot and garlic
spitting;
        they share serenity
                with the cross-legged
Chinese adolescent
        seated between them
                reading, and whose look
wears the tranquillity of consciousness
        forgotten in its object—
                his book
bears for a title
        SUCCESS
                in spelling.
How
        does one spell out this
                che penetra e risplende
from square
        into the hill-side alley-ways
                around it, where
between tall houses
        children of the Mediterranean
                and Chinese element
mingle
        their American voices? . . .
                The dictionary

defines idyllium
as meaning
'a piece, descriptive
chiefly of rustic life';
we
are in town: here
let it signify
this poised quiescence, pause
and possibility in which
the music of the generations
binds into its skein
the flowing instant,
while the winter sun
pursues the shadow
before a church
whose decoration
is a quotation from *Paradiso.*

SMALL ACTION POEM

for Robert and Bobbie Creeley

To arrive
unexpectedly
from nowhere:
then:
having done
what it was
one came for,
to depart.
The door
is open now
that before
was neither
open
nor was it there.
It is like
Chopin
shaking
music from the fingers,

making that
    in which
        all is either
technique
    heightened to sorcery
        or nothing but notes.
To arrive
    unexpectedly
        at somewhere
and the final
    chord, the final
        word.

SWIMMING CHENANGO LAKE

Winter will bar the swimmer soon.
  He reads the water's autumnal hesitations
A wealth of ways: it is jarred,
  It is astir already despite its steadiness,
Where the first leaves at the first
  Tremor of the morning air have dropped
Anticipating him, launching their imprints
  Outwards in eccentric, overlapping circles.
There is a geometry of water, for this
  Squares off the clouds' redundances
And sets them floating in a nether atmosphere
  All angles and elongations: every tree
Appears a cypress as it stretches there
  And every bush that shows the season,
A shaft of fire. It is a geometry and not
  A fantasia of distorting forms, but each
Liquid variation answerable to the theme
  It makes away from, plays before:
It is a consistency, the grain of the pulsating flow.
  But he has looked long enough, and now
Body must recall the eye to its dependence
  As he scissors the waterscape apart
And sways it to tatters. Its coldness
  Holding him to itself, he grants the grasp,

For to swim is also to take hold
  On water's meaning, to move in its embrace
And to be, between grasp and grasping, free.
  He reaches in-and-through to that space
The body is heir to, making a where
  In water, a possession to be relinquished
Willingly at each stroke. The image he has torn
  Flows-to behind him, healing itself,
Lifting and lengthening, splayed like the feathers
  Down an immense wing whose darkening spread
Shadows his solitariness: alone, he is unnamed
  By this baptism, where only Chenango bears a name
In a lost language he begins to construe—
  A speech of densities and derisions, of half-
Replies to the questions his body must frame
  Frogwise across the all but penetrable element.
Human, he fronts it and, human, he draws back
  From the interior cold, the mercilessness
That yet shows a kind of mercy sustaining him.
  The last sun of the year is drying his skin
Above a surface a mere mosaic of tiny shatterings,
  Where a wind is unscaping all images in the flowing obsidian,
The going-elsewhere of ripples incessantly shaping.

PROMETHEUS

Summer thunder darkens, and its climbing
  Cumulae, disowning our scale in the zenith,
Electrify this music: the evening is falling apart.
  Castles-in-air; on earth: green, livid fire.
The radio simmers with static to the strains
  Of this mock last-day of nature and of art.

We have lived through apocalypse too long:
  Scriabin's dinosaurs! Trombones for the transformation
That arrived by train at the Finland Station,
  To bury its hatchet after thirty years in the brain
Of Trotsky. Alexander Nikolayevitch, the events
  Were less merciful than your mob of instruments.

Too many drowning voices cram this waveband.
  I set Lenin's face by yours—
Yours, the fanatic ego of eccentricity against
  The systematic son of a schools inspector
Tyutchev on desk—for the strong man reads
  Poets as the antisemite pleads: 'A Jew was my friend.'

Cymballed firesweeps. Prometheus came down
  In more than orchestral flame and Kérensky fled
Before it. The babel of continents gnaws now
  And tears at the silk of those harmonies that seemed
So dangerous once. You dreamed an end
  Where the rose of the world would go out like a close in music.

Population drags the partitions down
  And we are a single town of warring suburbs:
I cannot hear such music for its consequence:
  Each sense was to have been reborn
Out of a storm of perfumes and light
  To a white world, an in-the-beginning.

In the beginning, the strong man reigns:
  Trotsky, was it not then you brought yourself
To judgement and to execution, when you forgot
  Where terror rules, justice turns arbitrary?
Chromatic Prometheus, myth of fire,
  It is history topples you in the zenith.

Blok, too, wrote The Scythians
  Who should have known: he who howls
With the whirlwind, with the whirlwind goes down.
  In this, was Lenin guiltier than you
When, out of a merciless patience grew
  The daily prose such poetry prepares for?

Scriabin, Blok, men of extremes,
  History treads out the music of your dreams
Through blood, and cannot close like this
  In the perfection of anabasis. It stops. The trees
Continue raining though the rain has ceased
  In a cooled world of incessant codas:

Hard edges of the houses press
  On the after-music senses, and refuse to burn,
Where an ice-cream van circulates the estate
  Playing Greensleeves, and at the city's
Stale new frontier even ugliness
  Rules with the cruel mercy of solidities.

A DREAM

or the worst of both worlds

Yevtushenko, Voznesensky and I
are playing to a full house: I lack their verve
(I know) their red reserve
of Scythian corpuscles, to ride in triumph through
Indianapolis. They read. Libido roars
across the dionysian sluice of the applause
and the very caryatids lean down
to greet them: youth towers (feet
on shoulders) into instant acrobatic pyramids—
human triforia to shore up the roof
cheering. I come on
sorting my pages, searching for the one
I've failed to write. It's October
nineteen seventeen once more. But is it me
or Danton from the tumbril, stentoriously
starts delivering one by one my bits of ivory?
No matter. I still ride their tide of cheers
and I could read the whole sheaf
backwards, breasting effortlessly
the surge of sweat and plaudits to emerge
laurelled in vatic lather, brother, bard:
they hear me out who have not heard one word,
bringing us back for bows, bringing down the house
once more. The reds return to their homeground stadia,
their unforeseen disgraces; I
to the sobriety of a dawn-cold bed, to own
my pariah's privilege, my three-inch spaces,
the reader's rest and editor's colophon.

A WORD IN EDGEWAYS

Tell me about yourself they
say and you begin to
tell them about yourself and
that is just the way I
am is their reply: they play
it all back to you in another
key, their key, and then in mid-
narrative they pay you a
compliment as if to say what a good
listener you are I am
a good listener my stay
here has developed my faculty I will
say that for me I will not
say that every literate male in
America is a soliloquist, a
ventriloquist, a strategic
egotist, an inveterate
campaigner-explainer over and
back again on the terrain of him-
self—what I will
say is they are not un-
interesting: they are simply
unreciprocal and yes it was a
pleasure if not an unmitigated
pleasure and I yes I did enjoy our
conversation goodnightthankyou

EDEN

I have seen Eden. It is a light of place
  As much as the place itself; not a face
Only, but the expression on that face: the gift
  Of forms constellates cliff and stones:
The wind is hurrying the clouds past,
  And the clouds as they flee, ravelling-out
Shadow a salute where the thorn's barb
  Catches the tossed, unroving sack

That echoes their flight. And the same
  Wind stirs in the thicket of the lines
In Eden's wood, the radial avenues
  Of light there, copious enough
To draft a city from. Eden
  Is given one, and the clairvoyant gift
Withdrawn, 'Tell us,' we say
  'The way to Eden', but lost in the meagre
Streets of our dispossession, where
  Shall we turn, when shall we put down
This insurrection of sorry roofs? Despair
  Of Eden is given, too: we earn
Neither its loss nor having. There is no
  Bridge but the thread of patience, no way
But the will to wish back Eden, this leaning
  To stand against the persuasions of a wind
That rings with its meaninglessness where it sang its meaning.

ADAM

Adam, on such a morning, named the beasts:
  It was before the sin. It is again.
An openwork world of lights and ledges
  Stretches to the eyes' lip its cup:
Flower-maned beasts, beasts of the cloud,
  Beasts of the unseen, green beasts
Crowd forward to be named. Beasts of the qualities
  Claim them: sinuous, pungent, swift:
We tell them over, surround them
  In a world of sounds, and they are heard
Not drowned in them; we lay a hand
  Along the snakeshead, take up
The nameless muzzle, to assign its vocable
  And meaning. Are we the lords or limits
Of this teeming horde? We bring
  To a kind of birth all we can name
And, named, it echoes in us our being.
  Adam, on such a morning, knew
The perpetuity of Eden, drew from the words
  Of that long naming, his sense of its continuance

And of its source—beyond the curse of the bitten apple—
  Murmuring in wordless words: 'When you deny
The virtue of this place, then you
  Will blame the wind or the wide air,
Whatever cannot be mastered with a name,
  Mouther and unmaker, madman, Adam.'

NIGHT TRANSFIGURED

Do you recall the night we flung
  Our torch-beam down in among
The nettle towers? Stark-white
  Robbed of their true dimension
Or of the one we knew, their dense
  World seemed to be all there was:
An immense, shifting crystal
  Latticed by shadow, it swayed from the dark,
Each leaf, lodged blade above blade
  In serrated, dazzling divisions.
What large thing was it stood
  In such small occurrence, that it could
Transfigure the night, as we
  Drew back to find ourselves once more
In the surrounding citadel of height and air?
  To see then speak, is to see with the words
We did not make. That silence
  Loud with the syllables of the generations, and that sphere
Centred by a millenial eye, all that was not
  There, told us what was, and clothed
The sense, bare as it seemed, in the weave
  Of years: we knew that we were sharers,
Heirs to the commonalty of sight, that the night
  In its reaches and its nearnesses, possessed
A single face, sheer and familiar
  Dear if dread. The dead had distanced,
Patterned its lineaments, and to them
  The living night was cenotaph and ceaseless requiem.

ASSASSIN

'The rattle in Trotsky's throat and his wild boar's moans'
(Piedra de Sol)

Blood I foresaw. I had put by
  The distractions of the retina, the eye
That like a child must be fed and comforted
  With patterns, recognitions. The room
Had shrunk to a paperweight of glass and he
  To the centre and prisoner of its transparency.

He rasped pages. I knew too well
  The details of that head. I wiped
Clean the glance and saw
  Only his vulnerableness. Under my quivering
There was an ease, save for that starched insistence
  While paper snapped and crackled as in October air.

Sound drove out sight. We inhabited together
  One placeless cell. I must put down
This rage of the ear for discrimination, its absurd
  Dwelling on ripples, liquidities, fact
Fastening on the nerve gigantic paper burs.
  The gate of history is straiter than eye's or ear's.

In imagination, I had driven the spike
  Down and through. The skull had sagged in its blood.
The grip, the glance—stained but firm—
  Held all at its proper distance and now hold
This autumnal hallucination of white leaves
  From burying purpose in a storm of sibilance.

I strike. I am the future and my blow
  Will have it now. If lightning froze
It would hover as here, the room
  Riding in the crest of the moment's wave,
In the deed's time, the deed's transfiguration
  And as if that wave would never again recede.

The blood wells. Prepared for this
  This I can bear. But papers
Snow to the ground with a whispered roar:
  The voice, cleaving their crescendo, is his
Voice, and his the animal cry
  That has me then by the roots of the hair.

Fleshed in that sound, objects betray me,
  Objects are my judge: the table and its shadow,
Desk and chair, the ground a pressure
  Telling me where it is that I stand
Before wall and window-light:
  Mesh of the curtain, wood, metal, flesh:

A dying body that refuses death,
  He lurches against me in his warmth and weight,
As if my arm's length blow
  Had transmitted and spent its strength
Through blood and bone; and I, spectred,
  The body that rose against me were my own.

Woven from the hair of that bent head,
  The thread that I had grasped unlabyrinthed all—
Tightrope of history and necessity—
  But the weight of a world unsteadies my feet
And I fall into the lime and contaminations
  Of contingency; into hands, looks, time.

AGAINST EXTREMITY

Let there be treaties, bridges,
  Chords under the hands, to be spanned
Sustained: extremity hates a given good
  Or a good gained. That girl who took
Her life almost, then wrote a book
  To exorcise and to exhibit the sin,
Praises a friend there for the end she made
  And each of them becomes a heroine.
The time is in love with endings. The time's
  Spoiled children threaten what they will do,

And those they cannot shake by petulance
  They'll bribe out of their wits by show.
Against extremity, let there be
  Such treaties as only time itself
Can ratify, a bond and test
  Of sequential days, and like the full
Moon slowly given to the night,
  A possession that is not to be possessed.

IN THE FULLNESS OF TIME

A letter to Octavio Paz

The time you tell us is the century and the day
  Of Shiva and Parvati: imminent innocence,
Moment without movement. Tell us, too, the way
  Time, in its fullness, fills us
As it flows: tell us the beauty of succession
  That Breton denied: the day goes
Down, but there is time before it goes
  To negotiate a truce in time. We met
Sweating in Rome and in a place
  Of confusions, cases and telephones: and then
It was evening over Umbria, the train
  Arriving, the light leaving the dry fields
And next the approaching roofs. As we slowed
  Curving towards the station, the windows ahead swung
Back into our line of vision and flung at us
  A flash of pausing lights: the future
That had invited, waited for us there
  Where the first carriages were. That hesitant arc
We must complete by our consent to time—
  Segment to circle, chance into event:
And how should we not consent? For time
  Putting its terrors by, it was as if
The unhurried sunset were itself a courtesy.

MUSIC'S TRINITY

Lugar de las nupcias impalpables
for Octavio and Marie-José

Motion: not things
moving, where the harp's
high swan
sailing out across
clear water
has all our ear.

Time: not the crabbed
clock's, but the force
and aggregation as the horns'
cumulae mass
rising to rob the sky
of silence.

Space: not between
but where: as,
out of a liquid
turbulence, a tremulousness gives place
to Atlantis.

LOGIC

A trailed and lagging grass, a pin-point island
Drags the clear current's face it leans across
In ripple-wrinkles. At a touch
It has ravelled the imaged sky till it could be
A perplexity of metal, spun
Round a vortex, the sun flung off it
Veining the eye like a migraine—it could
Scarcely be sky. The stones do more, until we say
We see there meshes of water, liquid
Nets handed down over them, a clear
Cross-hatching in the dance of wrinkles that
Re-patterns wherever it strikes.

So much for stones. They seem to have their way.
But the sway is the water's: it cannot be held
Though moulded and humped by the surfaces
It races over, though a depth can still
And a blade's touch render it illegible.
Its strength is here: it must
Account for its opposite and yet remain
Itself, of its own power get there.
Water is like logic, for it flows
Meeting resistance arguing as it goes:
And it arrives, having found not the quickest
Way, but the way round, the channel which
Entering, it may come to a level in,
Which must admit, in certain and crowding fusion,
The irrefutable strength which follows it.

THE WAY OF A WORLD

Having mislaid it, and then
  Found again in a changed mind
The image of a gull the autumn gust
  Had pulled upwards and past
The window I watched from, I recovered too
  The ash-key, borne-by whirling
On the same surge of air, like an animate thing:
  The scene was there again: the bird,
The seed, the windlines drawn in the sidelong
  Sweep of leaves and branches that only
The black and supple boughs restrained—
  All would have joined in the weightless anarchy
Of air, but for that counterpoise. All rose
  Clear in the memory now, though memory did not choose
Or value it first: it came
  With its worth and, like those tree-tips,
Fine as dishevelling hair, but steadied
  And masted as they are, that worth
Outlasted its lost time, when
  The cross-currents had carried it under.
In all these evanescences of daily air,
  It is the shape of change, and not the bare

Glancing vibrations, that vein and branch
   Through the moving textures: we grasp
The way of a world in the seed, the gull
   Swayed toiling against the two
Gravities that root and uproot the trees.

DESCARTES AND THE STOVE

Thrusting its armoury of hot delight,
   Its negroid belly at him, how the whole
Contraption threatened to melt him
   Into recognition. Outside, the snow
Starkened all that snow was not—
   The boughs' nerve-net, angles and gables
Denting the brilliant hoods of it. The foot-print
   He had left on entering, had turned
To a firm dull gloss, and the chill
   Lined it with a fur of frost. Now
The last blaze of day was changing
   All white to yellow, filling
With bluish shade the slots and spoors
   Where, once again, badger and fox would wind
Through the phosphorescence. All leaned
   Into that frigid burning, corded tight
By the lightlines as the slow sun drew
   Away and down. The shadow, now,
Defined no longer: it filled, then overflowed
   Each fault in snow, dragged everything
Into its own anonymity of blue
   Becoming black. The great mind
Sat with his back to the unreasoning wind
   And doubted, doubted at his ear
The patter of ash and, beyond, the snow-bound farms,
   Flora of flame and iron contingency
And the moist reciprocation of his palms.

THE QUESTION

Having misread the house, 'What
  Room is it,' she said, 'lies beyond
That?' And towards the door
  Which did not exist, leaned
The room of air, the thousand directions
  Ungoverned by any eye save one—
The blind house-wall, that for its two
  Centuries had faced away
From that long possession of the moon and sun,
  Room of the damasked changes where
Tonight, a pentecostal storm-light
  Flashed and died through its patternings
And each invisible scene replied
  In echo, tree-lash and water-voice
With the gift of tongues. In the room of storm
  Rain raked the confine with its dense
Volley, the old house staining
  Through wall and floor, as the sodden
Clamorous earth exuded, locked
  Round on its soundlessness, but turned
Towards her question: 'What
  Room is it lies beyond that?'

WEATHERMAN

Weather releases him from the tyranny of rooms,
  From the white finality of clapboard towns.
The migrations have begun: geese going
  Wake him towards dawn, as they stream south
Drawing the north behind them, the long threat
  That disquiets his blood. He rises and roams
In the grey house. In the dark
  Height, geese yelp like a pack
Hunting through space. Unseen, they drive the eye
  Of the mind the way they go, through the opal
Changes of dawn light on the light of snow.
  The sun looks full at the town, at each

House with its double fringe of icicles
  And their shadows. He can hear no more
The cries that had woken him, but through eyes
  That wincing away from it, blink back
The radiance that followed the flock, he drinks in
  Human his inheritance and retrieved his kin
With that clamour, this cold, those changes-to-come from skies
  Now a stained-glass blue in the whiteness of the weather.

ON THE PRINCIPLE OF BLOWCLOCKS

Three-way Poem

The static forces
of a solid body
and its material strength
derive from
not the quantity of mass:
an engineer would instance
rails or T beams, say
four planes constructed to
contain the same volume as
four tons of mass

not a ball of silver
but a ball of air
whose globed sheernesses
shine with a twofold glitter:
once with the dew and once
with the constituent bright threads
of all its spokes
in a tense surface
in a solid cloud of stars

The static forces
not a ball of silver
of a solid body
but a ball of air
and its material strength

whose globed sheernesses
derive from
shine with a twofold glitter:

not the quantity of mass:
once with the dew and once
an engineer would instance
with the constituent bright threads
rails or T beams, say
of all its spokes
four planes constructed to
in a tense surface
contain the same volume as
in a solid cloud of stars
four tons of mass

CLOUDS

How should the dreamer, on those slow
  Solidities, fix his wandering adagio,
Seizing, bone-frail, blown
  Through the diaphanous air of their patrols,
Shadows of fanfares, grails of melting snow?
  How can he hope to hold that white
Opacity as it endures, advances,
  At a dream's length? Its strength
Confounds him with detail, his glance falls
  From ridge to ridge down the soft canyon walls,
And, fleece as it may seem, its tones
  And touch are not the fleece of dream,
But light and body, spaced accumulation
  The mind can take its purchase on:
Cloudshapes are destinies, and they
  Charging the atmosphere of a common day,
Make it the place of confrontation where
  The dreamer wakes to the categorical call
And clear cerulean trumpet of the air.

WORDS FOR THE MADRIGALIST

Look with the ears, said Orazio Vecchi,
  Trusting to music, willing to be led
Voluntarily blind through its complete
  Landscape of the emotion, feeling beneath the feet
Of the mind's heart, the land fall, the height
  Re-form: Look with the ears—they are all
Looking with the eyes, missing the way:
  So, waiting for sleep, I look
With the ears at the confused clear sounds
  As each replenished tributary unwinds
Its audible direction, and dividing
  The branchwork of chime and counterchime
Runs the river's thick and drumming stem:
  Loud with their madrigal of limestone beds
Where nothing sleeps, they all
  Give back—not the tune the listener calls
But the measure of what he is
  In the hard, sweet music of his lack,
The unpremeditated consonances: and the words
  Return it to you over the ground-
Bass of their syllables, Orazio Vecchi:
  Hear with the eyes as you catch the current of their sounds.

ARROYO HONDO

Twice I'd tried
to pass the
bastard outside
of Arroyo Hondo:
each time, the same
thing: out he
came in a
wobbling glide
in that beat-up
pick-up, his
head bent
in affable accompaniment,

jawing at
the guy who sat
beside him: the third
time (ready
for him) I
cut out wide,
flung him
a passing look as I
made it: we almost
made it together
he and I: the same
thing, out he
came, all crippled speed
unheeding: I could not
retreat and what
did I see? I
saw them
playing at cards
on the driving seat.

BEFORE THE DANCE

at Zuni

The dance
is not yet
and when it will begin
no one says:
the waiting
for the Indian
is half the dance,
and so they wait
giving a quality
to the moment
by their refusal
to measure it:
the moment
is expansible
it burns
unconsumed
under the raw bulbs

of the dancing chamber:
the Navajo faces
wear
the aridity of the landscape
and 'the movement
with the wind
of the Orient and
the movement against
the wind
of the Occident'
meet
in their wrinkles:
they wait, sitting
(the moment)
on the earth floor
(is expansible)
saying very little
or sleep
like the woman
slipping along the wall
sideways
to wake
in the clangour of the pulse of time
at the beginning
drum . . .

A SENSE OF DISTANCE

The door is shut.
The red rider
no longer crosses the canyon floor
under a thousand feet of air.

The glance that fell
on him, is shafting
a deeper well:
the boughs of the oak are roaring
inside the acorn shell.

The hoofbeats—silent, then—
are sounding now
that ride
dividing a later distance.

For I am in England,
and the mind's embrace
catches-up this English
and that horizonless desert space
into its own, and the three there
concentrically fill a single sphere.

And it seems as if a wind
had flung wide a door
above an abyss, where all
the kingdoms of possibilities shone
like sandgrains crystalline in the mind's own sun.

THE INSTANCE

They do say said
the barber running
his cold shears
downwards and over
the neck's sudden
surprised flesh:
They do say frost
will flow in
through the gap of a hedge
like water, and go
anywhere and I
believe it. I believe
him—a gardener,
he knows. The tepid
day erases
his wisdom and he
is out of mind
until at night
I grope for a way
between darkness and door

and passing a hand
down over
a parked car's
roof feel
the finger tips
burn at the crystal
proof of a frost
that finding a hole
in the hedge
has flowed through like water.

THE FOX GALLERY

A long house—
the fox gallery you called
its upper storey, because
you could look down to see
(and did) the way a fox would
cross the field beyond
and you could follow out, window
to window, the fox's way
the whole length of the meadow
parallel with the restraining line
of wall and pane, or as far
as that could follow the sense of all
those windings. Do you remember
the morning I woke you with the cry
Fox fox and the animal
came on—not from side
to side, but straight
at the house and we craned
to see more and more, the most
we could of it and then
watched it sheer off deterred
by habitation, and saw
how utterly the two worlds were
disparate, as that perfect

ideogram for agility
and liquefaction flowed
away from us rhythmical
and flickering and
that flare was final.

COMPOSITION

for John Berger

Courbet might have painted this
gigantic head: heavy, yellow
petal-packed bloom of the chrysanthemum.

He would have caught the way
the weight of it looms from the cheap-green
vase this side the window it lolls in.

But he would have missed the space
triangled between stalk and curtain
along a window-frame base.

The opulence of the flower
would have compelled him to ignore
the ship-shape slotted verticals

of the door in the house beyond
dwarfed by the wand of the stem;
and the gate before it would not

have echoed those parallels to his eye
with its slatted wood, its two
neat side-posts of concrete.

The triangle compacts the lot: there
is even room in it for the black
tyre and blazing wheel-hub of a car

parked by the entrance. But the eye
of Courbet is glutted with petals
as solid as meat that press back the sky.

TO BE ENGRAVED ON THE SKULL OF A CORMORANT

across the thin
façade, the galleried-
with-membrane head:
narrowing, to take
the eye-dividing
declivity where
the beginning beak
prepares for flight
in a still-
perfect salience:
here, your glass
needs must stay
steady and your gross
needle re-tip
itself with reticence
but be
as searching as the sea
that picked and pared
this head yet spared
its frail acuity.

AUTUMN

The civility of nature overthrown, the badger must fight in the roofless colosseum of the burning woods.

The birds are in flight, and the sky is in flight, raced by as many clouds as there are waves breaking the lakes beneath it.

Does Tristan lie dying, starred by the oak leaves? Tristan is on horseback, in search, squat, with narrow eyes, saddleless, burner of cities.

The field mouse that fled from the blade, flattened by wheels, has dried into the shape of a leaf, a minute paper escutcheon whose tail is the leaf stalk.

Yet the worm still gathers its rings together and releases them into motion. . . . You too must freeze.

The horses of Attila scatter the shed foliage under the splashed flags of a camp in transit.

A truce: the first rime has not etched the last oak-shocks; the rivermist floats back from the alders and the sun pauses there.

Peace? There will be no peace until the fragility of the mosquito is overcome and the spirals of the infusoria turn to glass in the crystal pond.

These greens are the solace of lakes under a sun which corrodes. They are memorials not to be hoarded.

There will be a truce, but not the truce of the rime with the oak leaf, the mist with the alders, the rust with the sorrel stalk or of the flute with cold.

It will endure? It will endure as long as the frost.

SKULLSHAPES

Skulls. Finalities. They emerge towards new beginnings from undergrowth. Along with stones, fossils, flint keel-scrapers and spoke-shaves, along with bowls of clay pipes heel-stamped with their makers' marks, comes the rural detritus of cattle skulls brought home by children. They are moss-stained, filthy with soil. Washing them of their mottlings, the hand grows conscious of weight, weight sharp with jaggednesses. Suspend them from a nail and one feels the bone-clumsiness go out of them: there is weight still in their vertical pull downwards from the nail, but there is also a hanging fragility. The two qualities fuse and the brush translates this fusion as wit, where leg-like appendages conclude the skulls' dangling mass.

Shadow explores them. It sockets the eye-holes with black. It reaches like fingers into the places one cannot see. Skulls are a keen instance of this duality of the visible: it borders what the eye cannot make out, it transcends itself with the suggestion of all that is there beside what lies within the eyes' possession: it cannot be possessed. Flooded with light, the skull is at once manifest surface and labyrinth of recesses. Shadow reaches down out of this world of helmeted cavities and declares it.

One sees. But not merely the passive mirrorings of the retinal mosaic—nor, like Ruskin's blind man struck suddenly by vision, without memory or conception. The senses, reminded by other seeings, bring to bear on the act of vision their pattern of images; they give point and place to an otherwise naked and homeless impression. It is the mind sees. But what it sees consists not solely of that by which it is confronted grasped in the light of that which it remembers. It sees possibility.

The skulls of birds, hard to the touch, are delicate to the eye. Egg-like in the round of the skull itself and as if the spherical shape were the result of an act like glass-blowing, they resist the eyes' imaginings with the blade of the beak which no lyrical admiration can attenuate to frailty.

The skull of nature is recess and volume. The skull of art—of possibility—is recess, volume and also lines—lines of containment, lines of extension. In seeing, one already extends the retinal impression, searchingly and instantaneously. Brush and pen extend the search beyond the instant, touch discloses a future. Volume, knived across by the challenge of a line, the raggedness of flaking bone countered by ruled, triangular facets, a cowskull opens a visionary field, a play of universals.

THE CHANCES OF RHYME

The chances of rhyme are like the chances of meeting—
  In the finding fortuitous, but once found, binding:
They say, they signify and they succeed, where to succeed
  Means not success, but a way forward
If unmapped, a literal, not a royal succession;
  Though royal (it may be) is the adjective or region

That we, nature's royalty, are led into.
  Yes. We are led, though we seem to lead
Through a fair forest, an Arden (a rhyme
  For Eden)—breeding ground for beasts
Not bestial, but loyal and legendary, which is more
  Than nature's are. Yet why should we speak
Of art, of life, as if the one were all form
  And the other all Sturm-und-Drang? And I think
Too, we should confine to Crewe or to Mow
  Cop, all those who confuse the fortuitousness
Of art with something to be met with only
  At extremity's brink, reducing thus
Rhyme to a kind of rope's end, a glimpsed grass
  To be snatched at as we plunge past it—
Nostalgic, after all, for a hope deferred.
  To take chances, as to make rhymes
Is human, but between chance and impenitence
  (A half-rhyme) come dance, vigilance
And circumstance (meaning all that is there
  Besides you, when you are there). And between
Rest-in-peace and precipice,
  Inertia and perversion, come the varieties
Increase, lease, re-lease (in both
  Senses); and immersion, conversion—of inert
Mass, that is, into energies to combat confusion.
  Let rhyme be my conclusion.

THE END

All those who have not died have married.
  A Pompeian pause arrests
Merton beside his window, and the view
  Below is parkland, final as none
Could be, but the moment after she
  Whose name is on the card he holds
Has gone. The sliver of pasteboard framed
  By the great window, now, forever,
He is perfected in regret. Dalton
  Hailing the cab that will carry him

Out of the book, the motif on his lips
   (*So much for London, then*) for the last time,
The last chord chimes, tolling the solitudes
   Of the vast mind they moved in.
Such ends are just. But let him know
   Who reads his time by the way books go,
Each instant will bewry his symmetries
   And Time, climbing down from its pedestal
Uncrown the settled vista of his loss.
   Is it autumn or spring? It is autumn or spring.
Before door and window, the terrible guest
   Towers towards a famine and a feast.

ON WATER

'Furrow' is inexact:
no ship could be
converted to a plough
travelling this vitreous ebony:

seal it in sea-caves and
you cannot still it:
image on image bends
where half-lights fill it

with illegible depths
and lucid passages,
bestiary of stones,
book without pages:

and yet it confers
as much as it denies:
we are orphaned and fathered
by such solid vacancies:

ROWER

A plotless tale: the passing hours
  Bring in a day that's nebulous. Glazes of moist pearl
Mute back the full blaze of a sea,
  Drifting continually where a slack tide
Has released the waters. Shallows
  Spread their transparency, letting through
A pale-brown map of sandbanks
  Barely submerged, where a gull might wade
Thin legs still visible above its blurred reflection.
  It seems nothing will occur here until
The tide returns, ferrying to the shore its freshness,
  Beating and breaking only to remake itself
The instant the advancing line goes under.
  And nothing does. Except for the inching transformations
Of a forenoon all melting redundancies
  Just beyond eyeshot: the grey veils
Drink-in a little more hidden sunlight,
  Shadows harden, pale. But then
Out into the bay, towards deeper water,
  Sidles the rower, gaining speed
As he reaches it. Already his world
  Is sliding by him. Backwards
He enters it, eyes searching the past
  Before them: that shape that crowns the cliff,
A sole, white plane, draws tight his gaze—
  A house, bereft so it seems of time
By its place of vantage, high
  Over cleft and crack. When, as momentarily,
He steals a glance from it to fling
  Across his travelling shoulder, his eyes
Soon settle once more along that line
  Tilted towards the shoremark. And though the ripple
Is beneath him now—the pull and beat
  Unfelt when further in—he cuts athwart it
Making his way, to the liquid counterpulse
  Of blades that draw him outwards to complete
The bay's half-circle with his own. Muscle
  And bone work to that consummation of the will
Where satisfaction gathers to surfeit, strain
  To ease. Pleased by his exertions, he abandons them

Riding against rested oars, subdued
  For the moment to that want of purpose
In sky and water, before he shoots
  Feathering once more baywards, his face
To the direction the tide will take when
  Out of the coherent chaos of a morning that refuses
To declare itself, it comes plunging in
  Expunging the track of his geometries.

THE LIGHTHOUSE

The lighthouse is like the church of some island sect
  Who have known the mainland beliefs and have defected
Only to retain them in native purity
  And in the daily jubilation of storm and sea,
But adding every day new images
  To their liturgy of changes—each one
Some myth over and done with now
  Because sea has rebegotten land and land
The sea, and all is waiting to declare
  That things have never been praised for what they were,
    emerging
Along promontory on enfiladed promontory.

TWO POEMS ON TITLES PROPOSED BY OCTAVIO AND MARIE-JOSÉ PAZ

I LE RENDEZ-VOUS DES PAYSAGES

The promenade, the plage, the paysage
all met somewhere
in the reflection of a reflection
in midair: cars, unheard,
were running on water: jetplanes
lay on their backs
like sunbathers
in a submarine graveyard

about to resurrect into the fronds
of ghost-palms boasting
'We exist'
to the sea's uncertain mirrors
to the reversed clocktowers that had lost
all feeling for time
suspended
among the overlapping vistas
of promenade, plage, paysage.

II LA PROMENADE DE PROTÉE

Changing, he walks the changing avenue:
this blue and purple are the blue
and purple of autumn underwater:
they are changing to green and he
is changing to an undulated statue
in this sea-floor park
and does not know
if the iced green will undo him
or which are real
among the recollections that cling
to him and seem to know him:
and hears overhead the shudder of departing keels.

STONE SPEECH

Crowding this beach
are milkstones, white
teardrops; flints
edged out of flinthood
into smoothness chafe
against grainy ovals,
pitted pieces, nosestones,
stoppers and saddles;
veins of orange
inlay black beads:
chalk-swaddled babyshapes,
tiny fists, facestones

and facestone's brother
skullstone, roundheads
pierced by a single eye,
purple finds, all
rubbing shoulders:
a mob of grindings,
groundlings, scatterings
from a million necklaces
mined under sea-hills, the pebbles
are as various as the people.

VARIATION ON PAZ

Hay que . . . soñar hacia dentro y tambien hacia afuera

We must dream inwards, and we must dream
  Outwards too, until—the dream's ground
Bound no longer by the dream—we feel
  Behind us the sea's force, and the blind
Keel strikes gravel, grinding
  Towards a beach where, eye by eye,
The incorruptible stones are our witnesses
  And we wake to what is dream and what is real
Judged by the sun and the impartial sky.

THE COMPACT: AT VOLTERRA

The crack in the stone, the black filament
  Reaching into the rockface unmasks
More history than Etruria or Rome
  Bequeathed this place. The ramparted town
Has long outlived all that; for what
  Are Caesar or Scipio beside
The incursion of the slow abyss, the daily
  Tribute the dry fields provide

Trickling down? There is a compact
  To undo the spot, between the unhurried sun
Edging beyond this scene, and the moon,
  Risen already, that has stained
Through with its pallor the remaining light:
  Unreal, that clarity of lips and wrinkles
Where shadow investigates each fold,
  Scaling the cliff to the silhouetted stronghold.

Civic and close-packed, the streets
  Cannot ignore this tale of unshorable earth
At the town brink; furrow, gully,
  And sandslide guide down
Each seeping rivulet only to deepen
  The cavities of thirst, dry out
The cenozoic skeleton, appearing, powdering away,
  Uncovering the chapped clay beneath it.

There is a compact between the cooling earth
  And every labyrinthine fault that mines it—
The thousand mouths whose language
  Is siftings, whisperings, rumours of downfall
That might, in a momentary unison,
  Silence all, tearing the roots of sound out
With a single roar: but the cicadas
  Chafe on, grapevine entwines the pergola

Gripping beyond itself. A sole farm
  Eyes space emptily. Those
Who abandoned it still wire
  Their vines between lopped willows:
Their terraces, fondling the soil together,
  Till up to the drop that which they stand to lose:
Refusing to give ground before they must,
  They pit their patience against the dust's vacuity.

The crack in the stone, the black filament
  Rooting itself in dreams, all live
At a truce, refuted, terracing; as if
  Unreasoned care were its own and our
Sufficient reason, to repair the night's derisions,
  Repay the day's delight, here where the pebbles
Of half-ripe grapes abide their season,
  Their fostering leaves outlined by unminding sky.

I UNSTILL UNIVERSE

Unstill universe of gusts
of rays, of hours without colour, of perennial
transits, vain displays
of cloud: an instant and—
look, the changed forms
blaze out, millennia grow unstable.
And the arch of the low door and the step
worn by too many winters, are a fable
in the unforeseen burst from the March sun.

II VENERIS VENEFICA AGRESTIS

She springs from the ground-clinging thicket, her face
—gay now, now surly—bound in a black
kerchief, a shrivelled chestnut it seems: no fine fleece
the hair that falls loose, but a lock
of curling goat-hair; when she goes by
(is she standing or bending?) her gnarled and dark
foot is a root that suddenly juts from the earth and walks.
Be watchful she does not offer you her cup of bark,
its water root-flavoured that tastes of the viscid leaf,
either mulberry or sorb-apple, woodland fruit that flatters with
lies
the lips but the tongue ties.
She governs it seems
the force of rounding moons
that swells out the rinds of trees
and alternates the invincible ferments,
flow of the sap and of the seas. . . .
Pronubial, she, like the birds that bring
seeds from afar: arcane
the breeds that come of her grafting.
And the mud walls of the unstable
cottage where the nettle grows
with gigantic stalk, are her realms of shadows:
she ignites the kindlings in the furnaces of fable.

And round the door, from neighbouring orchard ground
the fumes that rise
are the fine, unwinding muslins of her sibiline vespers.
She appears in the guise
of the centipede among the darknesses
by water-wheels that turn
no more in the maidenhair fern.
She is the mask that beckons
and disappears, when the light
of the halfspent wicks
makes voracious the shadows in the room where
they are milling by night, working at the presses,
and odours of crushed olives are in the air,
kindled vapours of grapejuice; and lanterns come
swayed to the steps of hobnailed boots.
The gestures of those who labour
in the fields, are accomplices
in the plots she weaves:
the stoop of those who gather up dry leaves
and acorns . . . and the shoeless tread and measured bearing
under burdened head, when you cannot see
the brow or the olives of the eyes
but only the lively mouth . . . the dress
swathes tight the flanks, the breasts, and has comeliness—
passing the bough she leaves behind
an odour of parching . . .
or the gesture that raises the crock
renewed at the basin of the spring.
She bends, drawing a circle:
her sign sends forth
the primordial torrent out of the fearful earth
(and the foot that presses the irrigated furrow
and the hand that lifts
the spade—power of a different desire summons them now);
she draws strength
from the breaths of the enclosures,
the diffused cries, the damp and burning
straw of the litters, the blackened
branches of the vine, and the shadow that gives back
the smell of harnesses of rope and sack,
damp baskets, where who stands
on the threshold can descry
the stilled millstone, hoes long used to the grip of rural hands:
the rustic shade ferments with ancestral longings.

Rockroses, thistles, pulicaria, calaminths—scents
that seem fresh and aromatic, are
(should your wariness pall) the lures
of a spiral that winds-in all,
(night bites into silver
free of all alloy of sidereal ray) she will
blur in a fume of dust the gentle hill-curve.
Now, she's in daylight, one hand against an oak,
the other hangs loose—filthy and coaxing,
her dress black as a flue-brush . . .
and the sudden rush of wind
over the headland, sets at large, lets flow
in a flood a divine
tangle of leaves and flourishing bough.
The heat, too, promises, discloses
freshness, vigour of the breath that frees
peach and the bitter-sweet
odour of the flowering almond tree; under coarse leaf
are fleshy and violent mouths, wild offshoots,
between the ferns' long fans
obscure hints of mushroom growths,
uncertain glances of water glint through the clovers,
and a sense of bare
original clay is there
near where the poplar wakes unslakeable thirst
with its rustling mirages of streams
and makes itself a mirror of each breeze,
where, in the hill's shade,
steep sloping,
the valley grows
narrow and closes
in the mouth of a spring
among delicate mosses.
If, for a moment,
cloud comes to rest
over the hill-crest or the valley threshold,
in the living shade
the shaft of that plough now shows
which shakes which unflowers unleafs
the bush and the forest rose.

AT SANT' ANTIMO

Flanking the place,
a cypress
stretches itself, its surface
working as the wind
travels it in a continual
breathing, an underwater
floating of foliage
upwards, till
compact and wavering
it flexes a sinuous
tip that chases
its own shadow
to and fro
across the still
stone tower.

ARIADNE AND THE MINOTAUR

When Theseus went down
she stood alone surrounded
by the sense of what finality it was
she entered now: the hot rocks offered her
neither resistance nor escape, but ran
viscous with the image of betrayal:
the pitted and unimaginable face
the minotaur haunted her with
kept forming there
along the seams and discolorations
and in the diamond sweat
of mica: the sword and thread
had been hers to give, and she
had given them, to this easer of destinies:
if she had gone
alone out of the sun and down where he
had threaded the way for her,
if she had gone
winding the ammonite of space

to where at the cold heart
from the dark stone the bestial warmth
would rise to meet her
unarmed in acquiescence, unprepared
her spindle of packthread . . . her fingers felt now
for the image in the sunlit rock, and her ears
at the shock of touch took up a cry
out of the labyrinth
into their own, a groaning
that filled the stone mouth
hollowly: between the lips of stone
appeared he whom she had sent
to go where her unspeakable
intent unspoken had been to go
herself, and heaved unlabyrinthed at her feet
their mutual completed crime—
a put-by destiny, a dying
look that sought her
out of eyes the light extinguished,
eyes she should have led
herself to light: and the rays
that turned to emptiness in them
filling the whole of space with loss,
a waste of irrefutable sunlight spread
from Crete to Naxos.

HAWKS

Hawks hovering, calling to each other
   Across the air, seem swung
Too high on the risen wind
   For the earth-clung contact of our world:
And yet we share with them that sense
   The season is bringing in, of all
The lengthening light is promising to exact
   From the obduracy of March. The pair,
After their kind are lovers and their cries
   Such as lovers alone exchange, and we
Though we cannot tell what it is they say,
   Caught up into their calling, are in their sway.

And ride where we cannot climb the steep
  And altering air, breathing the sweetness
Of our own excess, till we are kinned
  By space we never thought to enter
On capable wings to such reaches of desire.

OF BEGINNING LIGHT

The light of the mind is poorer
than beginning light: the shades
we find pigment for
poor beside the tacit
variety we can all see
yet cannot say: of beginning light
I will say this, that it dispenses
imperial equality to everything
it touches, so that purple
becomes common wear, but purple
resolving in its chord
a thousand tones
tinged by a thousand
shadows, all
yielding themselves
slowly up: and the mind,
feeling its way among
such hesitant distinctions,
is left behind as they
flare into certainties that
begin by ending them
in the light of day.

CARSCAPE

Mirrored
the rear window
holds a glowing
almost-gone-day
scene, although the day
across this upland
has far to go: one drives
against its glare
that by degrees a moving
Everest of cloud
will shadow-over
while amid these
many vanishings
replenished, the wintry
autumnal afternoon
could still be dawn.

AUTUMN PIECE

Baffled
by the choreography of the season
the eye could not
with certainty see
whether it was wind
stripping the leaves or
the leaves were struggling to be free:

They came at you
in decaying spirals
plucked flung and regathered by the same
force that was twisting
the scarves of the vapour trails
dragging all certainties out of course:

As the car resisted it
you felt it in either hand
commanding car, tree, sky,
master of chances,
and at a curve was a red
board said 'Danger':
I thought it said dancer.

URLICHT

At the end of an unending war:
Horizons abide the deception
Of the sky's bright truce

But the dispersals have begun
There are no more roads
Only an immense dew

Of light
Over the dropped leafage
And in the room where

On the music-stand
The silent sonata lies
Open

APPEARANCE

Snow brings into view the far hills:
    The winter sun feels for their surfaces:
Of the little we know of them, full half
    Is in the rushing out to greet them, the restraint
(Unfelt till then) melted at the look
    That gathers them in, to a meeting of expectations
With appearances. And what appears
    Where the slant-sided lit arena opens

Plane above plane, comes as neither
    Question nor reply, but a glance
Of fire, sizing our ignorance up,
    As the image seizes on us, and we grasp
For the ground that it delineates in a flight
    Of distances, suddenly stilled: the cold
Hills drawing us to a reciprocation,
    Ask words of us, answering images
To their range, their heights, held
    By the sun and the snow, between pause and change.

THE NIGHT-TRAIN

composed
solely of carbon and soot-roses
freighted tight
with a million
minuscule statuettes
of La Notte (Night)
stumbles on
between unlit halts
till daylight begins
to bleed its jet
windows white, and the night-
train softly
discomposes, rose
on soot-rose,
to become—white
white white—
the snow-plough
that refuses to go.

EVENT

Nothing is happening
Nothing

A waterdrop
Soundlessly shatters
A gossamer gives

Against this unused space
A bird
Might thoughtlessly try its voice
But no bird does

On the trodden ground
Footsteps
Are themselves more pulse than sound

At the return
A little drunk
On air

Aware that
Nothing
Is happening

OVER ELIZABETH BRIDGE: a circumvention to a friend in Budapest

. . . my heart which owes this past a calm future.
(ATTILA JÓZSEF, *By the Danube*)

Three years, now, the curve of Elizabeth Bridge
Has caught at some half-answering turn of mind—
Not recollection, but uncertainty
Why memory should need so long to find
A place and peace for it: that uncertainty
And restless counterpointing of a verse
'So wary of its I', Iván, is me:

Why should I hesitate to fix a meaning?
The facts were plain. A church, a riverside,
And, launched at the further bank, a parapet
Which, at its setting-out, must swerve or ride
Sheer down the bulk of the defenceless nave,
But with a curious sort of courteousness,
Bends by and on again. That movement gave

A pause to thoughts, which overeagerly
Had fed on fresh experience and the sense
That too much happened in too short a time
In this one city: self-enravelled, dense
With its own past, even its silence was
Rife with explanations, drummed insistent
As traffic at this church's window-glass.

How does the volley sound in that man's ears
Whom history did not swerve from, but elected
To face the squad? Was it indifference,
Fear, or sudden, helpless peace reflected
In the flash, for Imre Nagy?—another kind
Of silence, merely, that let in the dark
Which closed on Rajk's already silenced mind?

Here, past is half a ruin, half a dream—
Islanded patience, work of quiet hands,
Repainting spandrels that out-arched the Turk
In this interior. These are the lands
Europe and Asia, challenging to yield
A crop, or having raised one, harvest it,
Used for a highroad and a battlefield.

The bridge has paid the past its compliment:
The far bank's statuary stand beckoning
Where it flows, in one undeviating span,
Across the frozen river. That reckoning
Which József owed was cancelled in his blood,
And yet his promise veered beyond the act,
His verse grown calm with all it had withstood.

IN MEMORIAM THOMAS HARDY

How to speak with the dead
so that not only
our but their
words are valid?

Unlike their stones,
they scarcely resist us,
memory adjusting
its shades, its mist:

they are too like their photographs
where we can fill
with echoes of our regrets
brown worlds of stillness.

His besetting word
was 'afterwards' and it released
their qualities, their restlessness
as though they heard it.

THE APPARITION

I dreamed, Justine, we chanced on one another
  As though it were twenty years ago. Your dark
Too vulnerable beauty shone
  As then, translucent with its youth,
Unreal, as dreams so often are,
  With too much life. 'Tomorrow',
You said, 'we plough up the pastureland.'
  The clear and threatening sky
New England has in autumn—its heightened blue,
  The promise of early snow—were proofs enough
Of the necessity, though of what pastureland
  You spoke, I'd no idea. Then
Reading the meaning in your face, I found
  Your pastureland had been your hallowed ground which now

Must yield to use. And all of my refusals,
  All I feared, stood countered
By the resolve I saw in you and heard:
  While death itself, its certain thread
Twisted through the skein of consequence
  Seemed threatened by the strength
Of those dead years. It was a dream—
  No more; and you whom death
And solitude have tried, must know
  The treachery of dreams. And yet I do not think it lied,
Because it came, without insistence,
  Stood for a moment, spoke and then
Was gone, that apparition,
  Beyond the irresolute confines of the night,
Leaving me to weigh its words alone.

JULIET'S GARDEN

J'ai connu une petite fille qui quittait son jardin bruyamment, puis s'en revenait à pas de loup pour 'voir comment il était quand elle n'était pas là.' (SARTRE)

Silently . . .
she was quieter than breathing now,
hearing the garden seethe
behind her departed echo:

flowers merely grew,
showing no knowledge of her:
stones hunching their hardnesses
against her not being there:

scents came penetratingly,
rose, apple, and leaf-rot,
earthsmell under them all,
to where she was not:

such presences could only
rouse her fears,
ignoring and perfuming
this voluntary death of hers:

and so she came rushing back
into her garden then,
her new-found lack
the measure of all Eden.

AGAINST PORTRAITS

How, beyond all foresight
or intention, light
plays with a face
whose features play with light:

frame on gilded frame,
ancestor on ancestor,
the gallery is filled
with more certainty than we can bear:

if there must be
an art of portraiture,
let it show us ourselves as we
break from the image of what we are:

the animation of speech, and then
the eyes eluding
that which, once spoken,
seems too specific, too concluding:

or, entering a sudden slant
of brightness, between dark and gold,
a face half-hesitant,
face at a threshold:

DURING RAIN

Between
slats of the garden
bench, and strung
to their undersides
ride clinging
rain-drops, white
with transmitted
light as the bench
with paint: ranged
irregularly
seven staves of them
shine out
against the space
behind: untroubled
by the least breeze they
seem not to move
but one
by one as if
suddenly ripening
tug themselves free
and splash
down to be
replaced by an identical
and instant twin:
the longer you
look at it
the stillness proves
one flow unbroken
of new, false pearls,
dropped seeds of now
becoming then.

ELEGY FOR HENRY STREET

for George and Mary Oppen

After the flight, the tired body
  Clung to the fading day of Henry Street:
There, it was hardly at an end, but midnight
  Weighed on the pulse of thought, its deep
Inconsistency working behind the eye
  That watched the lights come on—lights
Of the further shore, Manhattan's million
  Windows, floor on floor repeated
By the bay. I liked the street for its sordid
  Fiction of a small town order,
For its less and dingier glass
  As it let one down and back
Slowly out of transatlantic into human time,
  And its sooted bricks declared they were there
As they no longer are. 'Duck!' you cried, George,
  The day the militia filed out with rifles
At a Shriner celebration, but that was the pastoral era
  Of sixty-six, and how should we or they
Have known, as taps were blowing, and the echoes,
  Trapped in each scarred hallway
Meanly rhymed memory with civility,
  They were bugling the burial of a place and time?

From MOVEMENTS

I

I want that height and prospect such as music
  Brings one to—music or memory,
When memory gains ground drowned-out
  By years. I want the voyage of recovery,
The wind-torn eyrie and the mast-top
  Sight of the horizon island,
Look-out tower compounded from pure sound:
  Trough on trough, valley after valley
Opens across the waves, between the dancing
  Leaves of the tree of time, and the broken chords

Space a footing for melody, borne-out above
  The haven of its still begetting, the hill
Of its sudden capture, not disembodied
  But an incarnation heard, a bird-flight
Shared, thrust and tendon and the answering air.

VI *Written on Water*

One returns to it, as though it were a thread
  Through the labyrinth of appearances, following-out
By eye, the stream in its unravelling,
  Deep in the mud-flanked gash the years
Have cut into scarpland: hard to read
  The life lines of erratic water
Where, at a confluence of two ways
  Refusing to be one without resistance,
Shoulderings of foam collide, unskein
  The moving calligraphy before
It joins again, climbing forward
  Across obstructions: but do you recall
That still pool—it also fed its stream—
  That we were led, night by night,
To return to, as though to clarify ourselves
  Against its depth, its silence? We lived
In a visible church, where everything
  Seemed to be at pause, yet nothing was:
The surface puckered and drew away
  Over the central depth; the foliage
Kept up its liquid friction
  Of small sounds, their multiplicity
A speech behind speech, continuing revelation
  Of itself, never to be revealed:
It rendered new (time within time)
  An unending present, travelling through
All that we were to see and know:
  'Written on water', one might say
Of each day's flux and lapse,
  But to speak of water is to entertain the image
Of its seamless momentum once again,
  To hear in its wash and grip on stone
A music of constancy behind
  The wide promiscuity of acquaintanceship,
Links of water chiming on one another,
  Water-ways permeating the rock of time.

CURTAIN CALL

The dead in their dressing rooms
sweat out the sequel
through greasepaint and brocade.
O to have died
on the last note of a motif, flangeing home
the dovetails of sweet necessity . . . But the applause
draws them on to resurrection.
No one has won.
Time has undone the incurables
by curing them. The searoar of hands
throbbing, ebbing, each castaway
starts to explore his island. Vans
are standing outside now,
ready for palaces and caverns where
past hoardings and houses
boarded against demolition
a late-night traffic
turning its headlamps towards the peripheries gives
caller and called
back to their own unplotted lives.

AT STOKE

I have lived in a single landscape. Every tone
  And turn have had for their ground
These beginnings in grey-black: a land
  Too handled to be primary—all the same,
The first in feeling. I thought it once
  Too desolate, diminished and too tame
To be the foundation for anything. It straggles
  A haggard valley and lets through
Discouraged greennesses, lights from a pond or two.
  By ash-tips, or where the streets give out
In cindery in-betweens, the hills
  Swell up and free of it to where, behind

The whole vapoury, patched battlefield,
  The cows stand steaming in an acrid wind.
This place, the first to seize on my heart and eye,
  Has been their hornbook and their history.

THE MARL PITS

It was a language of water, light and air
  I sought—to speak myself free of a world
Whose stoic lethargy seemed the one reply
  To horizons and to streets that blocked them back
In a monotone fume, a bloom of grey.
  I found my speech. The years return me
To tell of all that seasoned and imprisoned:
  I breathe familiar, sedimented air
From a landscape of disembowellings, underworlds
  Unearthed among the clay. Digging
The marl, they dug a second nature
  And water, seeping up to fill their pits,
Sheeted them to lakes that wink and shine
  Between tips and steeples, streets and waste
In slow reclaimings, shimmers, balancings,
  As if kindling Eden rescinded its own loss
And words and water came of the same source.

CLASS

Those midland *a*'s
once cost me a job:
diction defeated my best efforts—
I was secretary at the time
to the author of *The Craft of Fiction*.
That title was full of class.
You had only to open your mouth on it
to show where you were born
and where you belonged. I tried

time and again I tried
but I couldn't make it
that top *A—ah*
I should say—
it sounded like gargling.
I too visibly shredded his fineness:
it was clear the job couldn't last
and it didn't. Still, I'd always thought him an ass
which he pronounced arse. There's no accounting for taste.

IN DECEMBER

Cattle are crowding the salt-lick.
The gruel of mud icily thickens.
On the farm-boy's Honda a sweat of fog drops.
They are logging the woodland, the sole standing crop.

From UNDER THE MOON'S REIGN

II FOXES' MOON

Night over England's interrupted pastoral,
   And moonlight on the frigid lattices
Of pylons. The shapes of dusk
   Take on an edge, refined
By a drying wind and foxes bring
   Flint hearts and sharpened senses to
This desolation of grisaille in which the dew
   Grows clearer, colder. Foxes go
In their ravenous quiet to where
   The last farm meets the first
Row from the approaching town: they nose
   The garbage of the yards, move through

The white displacement of a daily view
  Uninterrupted. Warm sleepers turn,
Catch the thin volpine bark between
  Dream on dream, then lose it
To the babbling undertow they swim. These
  Are the fox hours, cleansed
Of all the meanings we can use
  And so refuse them. Foxes glow,
Ghosts unacknowledged in the moonlight
  Of the suburb, and like ghosts they flow
Back, racing the coming red, the beams
  Of early cars, a world not theirs
Gleaming from kindled windows, asphalt, wires.

IV AFTER A DEATH

A little ash, a painted rose, a name.
  A moonshell that the blinding sky
Puts out with winter blue, hangs
  Fragile at the edge of visibility. That space
Drawing the eye up to its sudden frontier
  Asks for a sense to read the whole
Reverted side of things. I wanted
  That height and prospect such as music brings—
Music or memory. Neither brought me here.
  This burial place straddles a green hill,
Chimneys and steeples plot the distances
  Spread vague below: only the sky
In its upper reaches keeps
  An untarnished January colour. Verse
Fronting that blaze, that blade,
  Turns to retrace the path of its dissatisfactions,
Thought coiled on thought, and only certain that
  Whatever can make bearable or bridge
The waste of air, a poem cannot.
  The husk of moon, risking the whole of space,
Seemingly sails it, frailly launched
  To its own death and fulness. We buried
A little ash. Time so broke you down,
  Your lost eyes, dry beneath
Their matted lashes, a painted rose
  Seems both to memorialize and mock

What you became. It picks your name out
  Written on the roll beside a verse—
Obstinate words: measured against the blue,
  They cannot conjure with the dead. Words,
Bringing that space to bear, that air
  Into each syllable we speak, bringing
An earnest to us of the portion
  We must inherit, what thought of that would give
The greater share of comfort, greater fear—
  To live forever, or to cease to live?
The imageless unnaming upper blue
  Defines a world, all images
Of endeavours uncompleted. Torn levels
  Of the land drop, street by street,
Pitted and pooled, its wounds
  Cleansed by a light, dealt out
With such impartiality you'd call it kindness,
  Blindly assuaging where assuagement goes unfelt.

From FYODOR TYUTCHEV

THE PAST

(Tsarskoe selo—site of the imperial palace)

Place has its undertone. Not all
Is sun and surface.
There, where across the calm
Gold roofs stream in,
The lake detains the image:
Presence of past,
Breath of the celebrated dead.

Beneath the sun-gold
Lake currents glint . . .
Past power, dreaming this trance of consummation,
Its sleep unbroken by
Voices of swans in passing agitation.

A STORM, ON THE ROAD

The sun, unwilling and irresolute,
Looks fieldward. Listen:
A peal from the thunderhead. A passing
Frown on the earth's face.

Warm wind-gusts; the rain
Falling with hesitations; thunder
At a remove . . . Greening, the corn-crops
Under the storm loom greener.

There! —the blue of lightning
Cascades out of cloud, where fire
Distinct, white, flying
Has selvedged the borders.

Dust in a whirlwind flies
Upward, as the fields receive
The angrier force of drops
Enacting the thunder-threats.

From sun to field, once more
A misgiving glance:
And the whole earth, bewildered,
Drowns under radiance.

ENTERING AUTUMN

Entering autumn, there ensues
(Its beauty is in brevity)
A season of crystalline repose,
Still day with lucent dusk . . .

Steady incursion of the blade
Lets space into the crop:
Emptiness over all, save where
Cobweb on idle furrow
Stretches its gleam of subtle hair.

Birdless, the vacant atmosphere;
But the first tempests lie
Folded, as liquid, mild
Warm-blue keeps winter from the resting field.

AT VSHCHIZH

After the tumult and the blood
Had died, had dried,
Silence unmade its history:
A group of mounds; on them
A group of oaks. They spread
Their broad unmindful glories
Over the unheard rumour of those dead
And rustle there, rooted on ruin.
All nature's knowledge
Is to stay unknowing—
Ours, to confess confusion:
Dreamt-out by her,
Our years are apparitions in their coming-going.
Her random seed
Spread to their fruitless feat, she then
Regathers them
Into that peace all history must feed.

From ANTONIO MACHADO

LAMENT OF THE VIRTUES AND VERSES ON ACCOUNT OF THE DEATH OF DON GUIDO

It was pneumonia
finally carried away
Don Guido, and so the bells
(din-dan) toll for him the whole day.

Died Don Guido
gentleman; when younger
great at gallantry and roistering,
a minor talent in the bullring—
older, his prayers grew longer.

This Sevillan gentleman
kept (so they say)
a seraglio, was apt
at managing a horse
and a master
at cooling manzanilla.

When his riches dwindled
it was his obsession
to think that he ought to think
of settling in quiet possession.
And he settled
in a very Spanish way
which was—to marry
a maiden of large fortune
and to repaint his blazons,
to refer to the traditions of
'this house of ours',
setting a measure
to scandals and amours
and damping down the expenditure on pleasure.

He became, great pagan
that he was,
brother in a fraternity;
on Holy Thursday could be seen
disguised
(the immense candle in his hand)
in the long robe of a Nazarene.

Today
you may hear the bell
say that the good Don Guido
with solemn facc
tomorrow must go
the slow road to the burial place.
For ever and for always
gone, good Don Guido . . .

'What have you left?' some will say—
I ask, 'What have you taken
to the world in which you are today?'

Your love for braid
and for silks and gold
and the blood of bulls and the fume that rolled
from off the altars.

To good Don Guido and his equipage
bon voyage!

The here
and the there,
cavalier,
show in your withered face,
confess the infinite:
the nothingness.

Oh the thin cheeks
yellow
and the eyelids, wax,
and the delicate skull
on the bed's pillow!

Oh end of an aristocracy!
The beard on breast
lies limp and hoary,
in the rough serge
of a monk he's dressed;
crossed, the hands that cannot stir
and the Andalusian gentleman
on his best behaviour.

THE EPHEMERAL PAST

Habitué of a small-town club, this man
who saw Carancha poised one day
to take the bull,
has a withered skin, hair going grey,
eyes dim with disenchantment, and beneath
the grey moustache, lips bent
in nausea and a look
that's sad—yet sadness it is not
but something more, and less: the void
of the world in the hollow of his head. He still
sports a jacket coloured currant-red
in a three pile velvet, breeches
booted at their extremities and a caramel
Córdoba hat, turned and furbished well.
Three times he inherited, then lost the lot
three times at cards and twice
was widowed. An illegal round of chance
alone will make him brighten
sprawled at the green baize table;
once more the blood begins to flow
as he recollects a gambler's luck
or the afternoon of some torero,
drinks in an episode from the life
of a daring bandit of the road
or the bloody prowess of a knife.
He satirizes with a yawn the government's
reactionary politics and then
predicts the liberals will come to power
again, just as the stork returns to the bell-tower.
Something of a farmer still, he eyes
the heavens, fears them and at times will sigh
thinking of his olives and, disconsolate,
watches for weather-signs when rain is late.
For the rest, boredom. Taciturn, hypochondriac,
shut in the Arcadia of the present,
and to his brow
only the movement of the smoke gives now
its look of thought. This man is neither
of yesterday nor tomorrow
but of never. Hispanic stock, he's not
the fruit that grew to ripen or to rot,

but shadow-fruit
from a Spain that did not come to be,
that passed away, yet, dead
persists to haunt us with a greying head.

TO JOSÉ MARÍA PALACIO

Palacio,
good friend,
is spring
already clothing
the branches of the poplar trees
on road and river?
In the plain
of the upper Duero
spring
comes so slowly
but when she comes
she is all sweetness! . . .
The old elms,
have they
any new leaves?
As yet
the acacias will be bare,
and under snow
the mountains of the sierras.
Oh, there
in the sky of Aragon
the so beautiful
white and rose
mass of Moncayo!
Are the thorns
in flower among grey rocks
and are
white daisies there
in the delicate grass?
By now

storks will have been
arriving on those belfries.
There will be
greens of the coming wheat,
a going
of brown mules
into fields prepared for sowing
and of the peasants
who plant late crops
with the rains of April.
Already
bees
will broach
the thyme and rosemary.
Are plum trees
into blossom, do
violets
remain there too?
Stealthy,
with lures for the partridge
under a length of cloak,
huntsmen will not be absent.
Palacio,
good friend,
do the riverbanks
hold nightingales already?
On a blue
afternoon, the first
roses and first lilies
in the gardens,
go
climb Espino:
airy Espino where *her* country is.

From CÉSAR VALLEJO

TRILCE III

The grown-ups
what time are they coming back?
Blind Santiago is striking six
and already it's very dark.

She'd soon be home, mother said.

Aguedita, Nativa, Miguel,
watch out, don't go there where
griefs that double you up
have just gone by
whining their memories
towards the silent yard
and where the hens are still
getting settled, they were so scared.
Better if we stayed
here: she'd soon be home, mother said.

Besides, we should not
grieve. Let's go on
seeing the boats (mine's
the nicest of the lot!)
with which we play
the whole blessed day without a quarrel
as good children should: they've stayed
in the puddle, ready,
freighted with sweet things for tomorrow.

Obedient and resigned,
let's wait like this
for the return, the excuses
from the grown-ups—they
always the first to abandon
the small ones in the house,
as if it were us were unable to get away.

Aguedita, Nativa, Miguel?
I'm calling, feeling about
in the dark for you. Don't
go out and leave me
and I the only one shut in.

TRILCE XXIII

Glowing bakehouse of those my biscuits; pure
innumerable yolk of childhood, mother. Oh your four

birds' meals, astoundingly ill-bewailed
mother: your beggars. The last two
sisters, Miguel who died and me
still tugging a tress for each letter of the abc.

Morning and afternoon, in the upstairs
parlour, you doled us out shares
twice over, of time's rich
communion wafers, so that we
might have left to us
husks of watches, stopped punctually
in the going-round of the twenty-four.

Mother, and now! Now
in what small cavity would remain,
in what capillary shoot, a certain crumb
tied now to my throat
that doesn't want to go down. Now
that even your pure bones will become
flour, that there will be
nothing in which to knead,
tender honeyjar of loving-kindness!
even in the crude shadow, even in the big molar whose gum
throbs from that littlc milky rcccss
that carves itself forth and buds
unnoticed—you saw it so many times!—
in the closed hands newly born.

So the earth will hear
in your taciturnity, how they all
come collecting from us the rent of the world
where you leave us, and the price
of that interminable bread. And they
collect it from us, when we
being little then (as you would see)
could have snatched it away
from no one; when you gave it to us . . .
can you say
  little mother?

TRILCE LXI

I get down
  from the horse tonight,
before the door of the house, where
at cockcrow I took my leave.
It's shut and nobody answers there.

The stone bench, astraddle on which
Mother gave birth
to my elder brother
so that he might saddle
loins I had ridden bareback
by village lanes
and by garden walls, a child
of the village; the bench on which
I left to yellow in the sun
my painful childhood . . . And this
pain that imprints the title page?

A god in the alien peace,
the brute sneezes
as if also calling out;
it noses about
striking the pavement.
Soon, fears
make it hesitate; it neighs,
twitches alert ears.

Father must be awake
praying, and will think perhaps
I have been out late. My sisters
humming their illusions
simple, ebullient
in their work for the approaching feast
and now, almost nothing
is wanting. I wait
I wait, my heart
an egg in its moment
that obstructs itself.

Numerous family that we left
not long since,
nobody is keeping
watch today and not one
candle set on the altar
for our homecoming.

I call again . . . nothing.
Silent, we begin sobbing and the beast
neighs, neighs all the more.

They are all asleep for ever,
and so soundly
that, in the end, my horse
gets weary in turn
of nodding his head, and between
sleep lets fall
at each nod that it's all
right, everything
is all right.